THE BEDFORD SERIES IN HISTORY AND CULTURE

Pioneers of European Integration and Peace, 1945–1963

A Brief History with Documents

Sherrill Brown Wells

George Washington University

BEDFORD/ST. MARTIN'S Boston ♦ New York

For Bedford/St. Martin's

Publisher for History: Mary V. Dougherty
Executive Editor for History: Katherine Meisenheimer
Director of Development for History: Jane Knetzger
Developmental Editor: Margaret Manos
Editorial Assistant: Laurel Damashek
Production Supervisor: Jennifer Peterson
Production Associate: Maureen O'Neill
Senior Marketing Manager: Jenna Bookin Barry
Project Management: Books By Design, Inc.
Text Design: Claire Seng-Niemoeller
Indexer: Books By Design, Inc.
Cover Design: Elizabeth Tardiff
Cover Art: Jean Monnet and Some Members of the European Coal and Steel Community's High Authority Celebrated the Production of the First "European" Ingot of Steel, April 30, 1953. From left to right: Italian federalist Enzo Giacchero, Dutch diplomat Dirk Spierenburg, German trade unionist Heinz Potthoff, Belgian labor leader Paul Finet, Belgian economist Albert Coppé, Luxembourg diplomat Albert Wehrer, Jean Monnet, interpreter Ursula Wenmackers, and representative of Luxembourg's steel industry Félix Chomé. (*Copyright*: European Commission/Pol Aschman; *Source*: Médiathèque de la Fondation Jean Monnet pour l'Europe, Lausanne, Switzerland.)
Composition: Stratford Publishing Services, Inc.
Printing and Binding: RR Donnelley & Sons Company

President: Joan E. Feinberg
Editorial Director: Denise B. Wydra
Director of Marketing: Karen Melton Soeltz
Director of Editing, Design, and Production: Marcia Cohen
Manager, Publishing Services: Emily Berleth

Library of Congress Control Number: 2006930986

Manufactured in the United States of America.

2 1 0 9 8 7
f e d c b a

For information, write: Bedford / St. Martin's, 75 Arlington Street, Boston, MA 02116 (617-399-4000)

ISBN-10: 0-312-08616-4 (paperback)
1-4039-6809-8 (hardcover)
ISBN-13: 978-0-312-08616-9

Acknowledgments

Acknowledgments and copyrights are continued at the back of the book on page 168, which constitutes an extension of the copyright page.

Foreword

The Bedford Series in History and Culture is designed so that readers can study the past as historians do.

The historian's first task is finding the evidence. Documents, letters, memoirs, interviews, pictures, movies, novels, or poems can provide facts and clues. Then the historian questions and compares the sources. There is more to do than in a courtroom, for hearsay evidence is welcome, and the historian is usually looking for answers beyond act and motive. Different views of an event may be as important as a single verdict. How a story is told may yield as much information as what it says.

Along the way the historian seeks help from other historians and perhaps from specialists in other disciplines. Finally, it is time to write, to decide on an interpretation and how to arrange the evidence for readers.

Each book in this series contains an important historical document or group of documents, each document a witness from the past and open to interpretation in different ways. The documents are combined with some element of historical narrative—an introduction or a biographical essay, for example—that provides students with an analysis of the primary source material and important background information about the world in which it was produced.

Each book in the series focuses on a specific topic within a specific historical period. Each provides a basis for lively thought and discussion about several aspects of the topic and the historian's role. Each is short enough (and inexpensive enough) to be a reasonable one-week assignment in a college course. Whether as classroom or personal reading, each book in the series provides firsthand experience of the challenge—and fun—of discovering, recreating, and interpreting the past.

Lynn Hunt
David W. Blight
Bonnie G. Smith
Natalie Zemon Davis
Ernest R. May

Preface

After the disaster of the Second World War, Western European statesmen worked together to achieve what had eluded their predecessors after the First World War—a lasting peace. In the decade after 1945, under the initial leadership of French statesmen, six nations—Germany, Belgium, Italy, Luxembourg, the Netherlands, and France—took steps to increase their collaboration, and in 1957 agreed to gradually integrate their economies into a customs union and eventually a common market. As a result of this new European Economic Community (EEC), France and Germany, enemies in three wars since 1870, embarked on a process of economic integration. The reconciliation fostered by the EEC led these two nations to sign a treaty of friendship and cooperation in 1963.

The accomplishment of these visionary pioneers is significant not only because this peace has lasted for more than half a century but also because it was achieved by voluntary agreement of elected politicians—through negotiation, not war. The EEC attracted new members and laid the foundation for the creation of the European Union (EU) in 1992. Today the EU is recognized as an important international actor with great potential influence in promoting ethnic reconciliation and peace. This international organization, along with NATO, has been successful in furthering democracy, political stability, and the rule of law in Europe without the use of force. Its innovative institutions and policies have supported economic revitalization and conflict resolution on that continent.

This book explores the political risks taken by those farsighted leaders in the postwar period to heal the wounds of hostility and prevent another war. Designed for European history and European integration courses, as well as those focusing on conflict resolution, international organizations, and peace studies, it will help students understand how, in the second half of the twentieth century, effective international institutions brought enemies together to work for common interests. The introduction describes the evolution of European integration in the critical early years from 1945 to 1963 and concludes with a brief summary of developments between 1963 and 2006. Arranged chronologically, the documents in this text include memoirs, letters, speeches, official correspondence, memoranda, and declarations. They have been selected to illustrate the role, thinking, and motives of the most influential pioneers of European integration and the American and British leaders who supported that process.

Throughout this volume, plentiful readers' aids help students prepare for class discussions and writing assignments. Each document is introduced with a headnote, providing context for students' own analysis of the source. The appendixes include a glossary of terms and acronyms and a glossary of key figures for quick reference; a chronology of events and a list of questions for consideration to help students focus on the most important points raised by the readings; and a selected bibliography, which includes numerous suggestions for further explorations and online archival sources.

ACKNOWLEDGMENTS

I am deeply grateful to Charles Christensen, former president of Bedford/St. Martin's, for inviting me to write a book in this series and for his infinite patience with its slow birth. I wish to express my special gratitude to series editor Ernest May for initially suggesting the topic and later innovatively reshaping the focus of this book. I am also very grateful to Joan Feinberg, president of Bedford/St. Martin's, for her wholehearted support of this project. I am especially indebted to the late Henri Rieben, president of the Fondation Jean Monnet pour l'Europe in Lausanne, Claire Camperio-Tixier, head of the Multimedia Reference Library, and Françoise Nicod, head of the Archives, for providing me with documents and photos, and invaluable help at every stage; Hans-Peter Schwarz, Professor Emeritus, University of Bonn, and editor of the Adenauer Papers, Hans Peter Mensing, head of Research and Publishing, Chancellor Adenauer Fondation, and Klaus Schwabe, Aachen University, for their expert help with Adenauer's statements; Piero Graglia, University of Milan, for illuminating Spinelli; Gérard Bossuat, Université de Cergy-Pontoise, for wise counsel regarding the selection of documents; Alberta Spragia, University of Pittsburgh, for her thoughtful comments on an early draft; Phil

Wilkin, Archive of European Integration, for help with online archives; Lucinda Brown for designing the 1957 map; Paul Hurwit for translating Monnet's documents; and Harold Radday and Christian Ostermann, Woodrow Wilson International Center for Scholars, for their translations of Adenauer's statements. The librarians at George Washington University, David Ettinger and Wendall Kellar, and Ann Sweeney and Sergio Lopez at the EU Delegation Library, were always patient and very helpful. This volume benefited from the thoughtful comments of those who reviewed the work for Bedford/St. Martin's, especially Desmond Dinan, George Mason University; Thomas Schwartz, Vanderbilt University; George Sheridan, University of Oregon; Roberta Manning, Boston College; William Gray, Purdue University; and Thomas Saylor, Concordia University. It was a pleasure to work with the Bedford Series editorial group, who offered helpful advice and rendered invaluable assistance at every stage: Mary Dougherty, Jane Knetzer, Katherine Meisenheimer, Laurel Damashek, Shannon Hunt, and the production staff of Emily Berleth, Nancy Benjamin, and Barbara Jatkola. My greatest debt is to Margaret Manos, developmental editor, whose superb editing greatly improved the manuscript. To those who provided encouragement and help at critical stages along the way, I owe more thanks than I can express here: Richard Kuisel, Donald Lamm, Melinda Scrivner, Sue Wheeler, Toni Dorfman, John Gaddis, Bonnie Smith, Jenonne Walker, Samuel Williamson, Stanley Crossick, Renelle Gannon, Lucy Kaufman, Lauren Liers, Christopher Wells, and especially Samuel Wells.

Sherrill Brown Wells

Contents

APPENDIXES

Maps and Illustrations

MAPS

ILLUSTRATIONS

PART ONE

Introduction: The Pioneers of European Integration

World War II left Europe shattered. Six years of catastrophic conflict had caused far greater damage and loss of life than any previous war. More than thirty-five million people perished, the greater portion of them civilians, and the economies of Germany, France, Britain, and the Soviet Union were destroyed. Round-the-clock bombing left cities in ruin and millions homeless. Industries were demolished, railways wrecked, bridges broken, and roads were blocked by rubble. Swollen corpses filled the tunnels and canals, and acute food shortages threatened starvation as rats multiplied and wild pigs roamed. By the end of 1945, Europe was in a state of social, political, and economic collapse.

The devastation of two world wars and their destruction of Europe as an economic power stimulated new thinking among the European leaders who emerged from the ashes of 1945. Haunted by the horrors of war and the humiliation of German aggression and occupation, these statesmen determined never to repeat the mistakes of their predecessors and began to focus on the problems of preventing another war. They believed they had no choice but to reexamine their existing institutions and societies. Europe's new leaders concluded that a foundation for a lasting peace was possible only through increased international cooperation and greater European unity.

WAR'S AFTERMATH: PLANS FOR PEACE, COLD WAR, AND RECONSTRUCTION

The idea of a united Europe as a means to preserve peace goes back to the thirteenth century, when prominent Christian and lay leaders promulgated a federation of European states as a defense against threats of military conquest, Turkish invasion, and political fragmentation. Later, during the eighteenth century, Enlightenment philosophers debated European unity, with some calling for European federation while others advocated a commonwealth of states. In the nineteenth century, advocates of peace proposed a "United States of Europe" as well as other forms of regional economic integration.[1]

The idea of European integration and cooperation continued to percolate during the early twentieth century, especially after World War I. In a speech before the League of Nations in 1929, French prime minister Aristide Briand proposed a new, confederal bond—that is, a league or alliance of nations created to work toward a common goal—among European peoples. A year later, he circulated a call for a permanent political committee and secretariat to form a union of governments within the framework of the League of Nations. As the first official endorsement of the idea of integration, the Briand Memorandum stimulated a flood of proposals, including a socialist federation of European states. But none of these schemes attracted widespread attention or support.[2]

The dire economic conditions at the end of 1945 and throughout 1946 once again stimulated Western Europeans to propagate various forms of international cooperation and collaboration. The deteriorating conditions heightened fears of a revived Germany, Soviet encroachment, and the spread of communism. Among the strongest advocates of European integration was the Italian Altiero Spinelli, a former resistance fighter who claimed that nationalism was the root of European conflict and scorned interwar leaders for their ineptitude and lack of foresight. Calling for drastic changes, Spinelli argued that a united Europe was essential to revitalize it and prevent a third world war (Document 1).

The cold war after World War II underscored the urgency of cooperation across national borders. In 1946, the mutual distrust and hostility between the United States and the Soviet Union, the two postwar superpowers, intensified into a geopolitical conflict between polarizing ideologies, competing economic systems, and a contest for control of Europe. While the East-West competition fell short of full-scale war (thus its designation as a "cold" war), it nevertheless developed into a massive arms race. Each superpower struggled to maintain its sphere of influence. Each was convinced that the other had aggressive intentions to control Europe through control of Germany. Under the dictator Joseph Stalin, the Soviet Union occupied Rumania, Bulgaria, and Hungary in 1944–1945 and installed subservient regimes in the Baltic states, in Poland, and then throughout the rest of Eastern Europe (see Map 1). Stalin saw the world as divided into two camps: imperialist, capitalist regimes pitted against Communist, progressive ones. His grand vision was Soviet domination of Europe. In 1946, Britain's rotund, eloquent wartime prime minister, Winston Churchill, delivered a powerful indictment of Stalin's postwar policy, warning that "an iron curtain" had "descended across the Continent" (Document 4).

At the end of the war, the victorious allies divided Germany into four zones of occupation—American, French, Soviet, and British—to be jointly administered by the Allied Control Council. Almost immediately, the Soviet Union refused to cooperate, fought over reparations, and imposed its authority on its zone, East Germany, through the Communist-dominated Socialist Unity party, which was under Soviet control. To counter Stalin's moves, the Western powers quickly consolidated their three zones into one, seeking to preserve as much of Germany, as possible under Western rule. Gradually, they began to allow limited self-government for the Germans in their zones, including the election of state legislatures, the creation of constitutional conventions, and the gradual resurrection of political parties in 1946. These reciprocal actions by the former wartime allies generated a growing sense of insecurity and reinforced suspicions in Washington and Moscow. Since the United States already possessed the atomic bomb, the Soviet leader felt compelled to acquire that capability as well. When he succeeded in 1949, both sides began to live in fear of surprise nuclear attack by the other.[3]

Western European leaders also feared the political appeal of the Communists in their own countries, as reflected in the large popular votes received by the French, Belgian, and Italian Communist parties in the 1946 elections. At first, the postwar coalition governments in these nations included Communists. But when they were ousted from government cabinets in 1947, the Communists and their supporters protested vigorously with strikes, lockouts, and riots. Western European statesmen, recognizing the attraction of communism to citizens facing starvation, poverty, and dislocation, also recognized the urgent need to diminish political instability at home.[4]

Map 1. *Soviet Territorial Expansion in Europe, 1945–1948*

Source: Martin Gilbert, *Routledge Atlas of Russian History*, Third Edition, ISBN 0415281199.

The Marshall Plan

As economic conditions worsened in Western Europe in 1946 and early 1947, Turkey and Greece were threatened by increased Soviet influence. In response, U.S. president Harry Truman announced a $400 million program of military and economic assistance to those nations. In March 1947, he pledged his support for "free peoples who are resisting attempted subjugation" and argued that world peace was necessary for American security (Document 6). The Truman Doctrine, approved by the U.S. Congress within two months, implied an American commitment to assist other, similarly threatened nations.[5]

Western Europe's economic deterioration had become alarming in 1947. Growing shortages of food, coal, fertilizer, and agricultural machinery combined with one of the harshest winters on record to limit spring harvests and production severely. Governments had difficulty financing food imports, and U.S. loans and other aid to France, Italy, and Britain had dried up. For U.S. secretary of state George Marshall, the failure of the wartime allies to finalize German and Austrian peace treaties at their Council of Foreign Ministers meeting in April was the turning point. He returned home convinced that the Soviets were trying to force an economic breakdown in Europe. In June, Marshall announced his grand strategy for reversing the desperate conditions that led Europeans to elect Communists to office—a long-term plan to assist Europe economically[6] (Document 7). Moscow sharply criticized the plan (Document 8). In early 1948, the Soviet Union's overthrow of the democratically elected government in Prague and its pressure on Finland to join a Soviet alliance reinforced the U.S. government's determination to help European countries rebuild their economies. The Marshall Plan legislation, the Foreign Assistance Act of 1948, officially known as the Economic Cooperation Act, passed Congress on March 30 and was signed by President Truman on April 1, 1948.[7]

The Marshall Plan, consisting of economic assistance to France, Germany, Belgium, the Netherlands, and twelve other Western European nations, influenced not just European recovery but European integration as well. The terms of the program required that nations receiving aid design and plan their economic activities collectively. Therefore, in April 1948, representatives from each of the countries receiving Marshall Plan aid created the Organization for European Economic Cooperation (OEEC). Although the OEEC failed to develop a comprehensive European recovery program as some American officials had hoped, it did foster new modes of thinking, and it encouraged the liberalization of trade and other ideas for achieving closer integration[8] (Document 11).

Revitalizing the French Economy

The political, economic, and intellectual leaders who emerged in France after the war agreed that drastic changes were needed to reconstruct and renovate the economy, improve French security, and restore the nation as a principal European industrial power (Document 2). However, they lacked both a strategy and the money to finance it. Jean Monnet, an international financier, innovative diplomat, and entrepreneurial cognac salesman, devised a pragmatic solution. Since Washington required detailed economic plans from nations seeking further economic aid, Monnet proposed in August 1945 to design an economic program that would both modernize France and allow it to obtain more U.S. funds. Provisional president Charles de Gaulle, who shared Monnet's goal of restoring war-torn France to a position of influence in Europe, accepted his proposal (Document 3). In January 1946, the French government authorized Monnet to develop his investment plan for simultaneous reconstruction and modernization and named him head of the new Planning Commission.

Monnet's able team devised a pragmatic economic plan called the Monnet Plan. Goals for the 1947–1950 period included developing national production and foreign trade, increasing productivity, ensuring full employment, raising the standard of living, and improving the conditions of national life. To allocate scarce resources, the Planning Commission designated six industries for immediate investment priority: coal mining, electricity, transportation, iron and steel, cement works, and agricultural machinery[9] (Document 9).

The planners viewed heavy industry—with a strong base in energy and steel—as the foundation of economic might, and they particularly wanted to make France more competitive in relation to Germany. Because they sought national self-sufficiency, their plan emphasized France's own resources, coal and hydroelectric power, rather than imported oil and gas. However, acute coal shortages and the terrible condition of the French mines right after the war meant greater dependence on foreign sources.[10] Since the steel industry depended on coke, the French needed to secure access to German coke as well as to coal supplies in the Ruhr Valley. Germany's coal-rich Saar province had been placed under French economic control after the war, and the French government hoped to retain it.[11]

From 1947 to 1950, the Planning Commission largely determined France's economic policy. Despite a rapid turnover of administrations, these men provided stability and continuity in its implementation. The planners met with business and labor leaders, managed reconstruction, allocated credits, and levied taxes to enforce their decisions. They tackled the major obstacles to their plan—rising inflation and inadequate funds—by persuading the government to take exceptional measures to reduce inflation and ensuring that much of the Marshall Plan aid from the United States went directly to the industries designated by their plan. As a result, from 1948 on, the French economy overall grew 5 percent a year, and by early 1950, it had stabilized. Despite some miscalculations, Monnet and his team of planners succeeded in launching postwar recovery and establishing the foundation for a more modern, competitive economy. This success increased Monnet's prominence in government circles and European capitals and enabled him and the French government to shape the postwar settlement in 1950 by proposing the first concrete steps toward European integration.[12]

Integration Schemes Proliferate

While European leaders proclaimed the need for political union, there was little agreement on what form this should take. Very few advocated a strong federation or shared sovereignty (Document 12). However, because Europe shared a cultural identity, many believed that some form of solidarity might pave the way to longer-lasting peace.

Churchill expressed the visions of many integrationists when he called for a United States of Europe in Zurich in 1946 (Document 5). Churchill did not believe that Britain needed to be part of such a united continent, but his call inspired others to create the International Committee of the Movements for European Unity in 1947, which organized a congress to publicize the idea of union and establish an institutional structure for a European organization. As a result of their work, the Congress of Europe, held in The Hague in May 1948, attracted several hundred delegates from sixteen nations. Its deliberations produced few practical measures, only strong statements about the need for a united Europe and some common institutions to support it (Document 14).

At the Congress of Europe, Churchill's proposal for a European assembly gained the support of Paul-Henri Spaak, the popular, vivacious prime minister of Belgium. Spaak had spent the war years exiled in London. After 1945, he was variously Belgium's prime minister and foreign minister, sometimes simultaneously, and a firm believer in European integration. His initiatives eventually led to the Treaty of Westminster, signed by ten nations on May 5, 1949, creating the Council of Europe. This new body, with Spaak as president of its Consultative Assembly, was the first postwar political organization of Western European states.[13]

Differences among the nations about the future shape of a united Europe limited the council's ability to advance European union (Document 15). Compromises made to accommodate Britain's insistence that the council's power remain limited prevented it from becoming an effective motor of integration. Nonetheless, the Council of Europe remains today an organization promoting European cultural unity, democracy, and human rights.[14]

While American aid stimulated European economic recovery and cooperation, Western European nations became increasingly fearful of renewed German aggression, the perceived Soviet threat from without, and the agitation of Communist political parties from within (Document 10). Although Britain and France had expanded their 1947 Treaty of Dunkirk to the Treaty of Brussels in March 1948, which included Belgium, Luxembourg, and the Netherlands, this agreement was directed against German, not Soviet, aggression. Feeling a need for U.S. involvement in a collective security system against the Soviet Union, European leaders appealed to the United States for a formal military alliance. In April 1949, representatives of twelve states, including Canada and the United States, agreed to enter into a military arrangement for the collective defense of Western Europe. The North Atlantic Treaty Organization (NATO) was a defensive alliance, which was viewed by the United States as part of a wider strategy of containing communism. NATO's institutional framework permitted continuous military as well as political consultation and provided its Western European member governments with experience in collective decision making. Along with the Marshall Plan, NATO provided increased political and economic stability and enhanced regional security for the European governments.[15]

FRENCH-GERMAN RAPPROCHEMENT

The Schuman Plan arose out of the critical nature of Franco-German relations in 1949–1950. The complex question of the status of Germany in the postwar world was colored by the long history of bitter conflicts between the French and German peoples dating back to 1870, and the memory of the fall of France in 1940 and German occupation was still a fresh wound. For France, the issue involved its reliance on German resources, notably coal, for its own economic revival (Document 13). For the Germans themselves, their neighbors, and the United States, the key issue was how to restore Germany's economic potential without a return to German hegemony. The United States viewed Germany as vital to the European as well as the world balance of power and pressed the NATO nations to integrate Germany into that evolving military alliance. Tension between the Western powers and the Soviet Union increased in April 1947 with the breakdown of negotiations over the Allied occupation of Germany. Strained relations were further aggravated by the Communist coup in Prague in February 1948, the Soviet Union's blockade of Berlin the following summer, and threats of Soviet encroachment and subversion elsewhere in Europe. As a result, Germany's status became a major stake in the cold war rivalry.[16]

Preventing another war from ravaging Europe had long preoccupied Jean Monnet, and in 1949 he understood that France's security and economic recovery required a new approach to West Germany. Since that nation had become the centerpiece in the cold war, he realized that West Germany's rapid recovery might raise the prospect of a renewed arms race and the specter of war (Document 16). With these concerns in mind, he devised a plan for France and West Germany to share coal and steel resources and markets. Without these German resources, France's steel industry would not recover, and French reconstruction would be handicapped. Monnet was also motivated by opposition to the reestablishment of German cartels (organizations formed to regulate prices and output), which he thought might stifle French industry. Monnet believed that by sharing resources and having access to the valuable German coal in the Ruhr region, the French would lose their fear of German industrial domination and thereby remove the greatest obstacle to a united Europe. A united Europe guided by a strong France, in Monnet's eyes, was the only long-term guarantee of peace.[17]

Monnet presented his strategy to French foreign minister Robert Schuman in April 1950. He advised Schuman that the Americans would proceed with West Germany's rehabilitation without France if they had to, and he underscored Germany's demand to increase its steel production. He argued that the U.S. policy of "containing" the Soviet Union dictated that the new West German state be "integrated" as part of Western Europe so that it could no longer threaten the West.

Schuman seized Monnet's plan as a way to advance his own goal, reconciliation between France and West Germany. This distinguished jurist, devout Roman Catholic, and French parliamentarian realized the need for a change in French postwar policy toward Germany, which depended on a weak Germany as well as American support. Schuman and the other foreign ministers of the Western occupying powers had begun to meet every few months, and he felt pressed to demonstrate to the Americans that Europe was willing to take collective steps to overcome some of its problems. Schuman provided the political leadership needed to win approval of the plan from the French and West German governments. On May 9, 1950, he announced the Schuman Plan (Document 17). He proposed that France and Germany enter negotiations to pool their coal and steel resources and markets. The common market for coal and steel thus created would be directed by a single institution composed of individuals appointed by the member governments, who would regulate these sectors by executive decision. Officials in Washington and Brussels hailed the plan (Documents 18, 20, and 21). Schuman assumed responsibility for tackling the question of the Saar province and appointed Monnet to head the negotiations that would lead to the creation of a common market for coal and steel. Monnet traveled to Bonn in mid-May to assure Konrad Adenauer (see Figure 1), first chancellor of the Federal Republic of Germany (West Germany), that the Germans would be treated as equals in the negotiations and to explain his vision of European unification (Document 19).

Adenauer, like Schuman, had a genuine personal yearning for Franco-German reconciliation. This experienced, crafty Catholic politician and former mayor of Cologne, main city of the Rhineland, had survived Nazi arrests and escaped from prison. Adenauer believed that the only way for Germany to regain international respectability was through cooperation with France, and he was eager to confirm that the West German government had no desire to achieve a new German supremacy. He also knew that the Franco-German core was essential to strengthen Western Europe against the Soviet Union. His pro-American views were not common among German politicians. However, Adenauer foresaw that only by integrating closely with its Western European neighbors could West Germany hope to remove the controls imposed by the occupying powers on its domestic and foreign policy. He also realized that integration provided

Figure 1. *Jean Monnet (left) and Konrad Adenauer, Strasbourg, September 10–11, 1952*

Pioneers Jean Monnet and Konrad Adenauer, Strasbourg, September 10–11, 1952, were attending the first meeting of the Common Assembly of the Coal and Steel Community, the first international assembly in Europe with legally guaranteed powers. Monnet and Adenauer earned each other's respect at their first meeting in Bonn, May 23, 1950, when Monnet won the German Chancellor's support for the Schuman Plan.

Copyright: Stiftung Bundeskanszler-Adenauer-Haus, Bad Honnef, Germany; *Source:* Médiathèque de la Fondation Jean Monnet pour l'Europe, Lausanne, Switzerland.

protection against further German aggression. Adenauer understood that the West Germans would be forced to accept the new organization's decisions on major issues of production, quotas, prices, and markets, and he had no objections to experimenting with a coal and steel community.[18]

Negotiations began in June 1950. France, Germany, Italy, Luxembourg, the Netherlands, and Belgium all agreed to accept the principle of supranationality, the idea that decisions made by majority vote of the six nations would govern the common market; no one nation's veto could block them. The contentious discussions over the next eight months proved very difficult, especially for the Germans, and almost failed. Adenauer faced harsh criticism at home from Kurt Schumacher, leader of the opposition Social Democratic party (SPD), who attacked the Schuman Plan on nationalistic and ideological grounds and charged Adenauer with putting the economic strength of Germany "in the service of French diplomacy."[19] The SPD feared the new arrangements would perpetuate the division of Germany and lead to rearmament, thus making reconciliation with other European countries extremely difficult. Concerned about the future status of the Ruhr, German industrialists resisted the proposed breakup of the cartels that regulated coal and steel prices and output.

Meanwhile, the French wrestled with U.S. pressure to see Germany rearmed. Suspicions that Stalin had instigated the outbreak of the Korean War in June 1950 heightened U.S. anxiety about increased Soviet military power and its intentions in Europe. Since the United States was concerned that it might not be able to deter Soviet aggression in central Europe while fighting in Korea, Washington wanted to rearm West Germany so that it could contribute to the common defense of Europe against the Soviets.[20]

French opposition to German rearmament threatened the delicate balance necessary for the Schuman negotiations to succeed. In reply, Monnet proposed to permit gradual German rearmament within a larger European army under a supranational European defense community (EDC) headed by a minister of defense (Document 22). Adopted by French prime minister René Pleven and endorsed by the National Assembly in October 1950, Monnet's scheme became known as the Pleven Plan (Document 23). Although heated debates about this new French initiative ensued in both Paris and Bonn, the Schuman negotiations ended successfully after John McCloy, U.S. high commissioner for West Germany, pressured Adenauer to ignore opposition from the SPD and German industrialists and consent to the agreement. The Treaty of Paris, signed on April 18, 1951, established the European Coal and Steel Community (ECSC), a supranational community aiming to establish a common market in coal and steel, free of customs duties and other trade restrictions.[21] It was ratified by six nations: France, West Germany, Italy, the Netherlands, Belgium, and Luxembourg.

British leaders, who viewed the ECSC as a threat to their national sovereignty, had declined to participate in the negotiations. They assumed that close involvement in the process of European integration would jeopardize Britain's ties to its current and former colonies, loosely united in the Commonwealth of Nations. British foreign secretary Ernest Bevin also resented not being consulted by Schuman before his announcement. The British government, therefore, never carefully assessed the Schuman Plan.[22]

The European Coal and Steel Community: A Supranational Community

With the support of the leaders of "the Six," Monnet began in the summer of 1952 to develop the functional economic community he had been so instrumental in designing. He was named president of the High Authority, the decision-making arm of the ECSC. In his inaugural address on August 10 in Luxembourg, he declared that despite being "incapable of eliminating our national antagonisms," the signatories had established "the first European Community, merging part of its members' sovereignty and subordinating it to the common interest." He also stated his belief that the High Authority had a "mandate" to make decisions binding for the Six. The High Authority's nine members, all chosen by their governments—two representatives from Italy, France, and Germany, and one from each of the other three countries—began the daunting challenge of creating this new community and its institutions. They tackled the gargantuan task of creating the High Authority's administrative structure, establishing departments, allocating duties, adopting rules of procedure and budget plans, and developing harmonization measures and ways to collect levies. These and many other decisions, such as to have four official languages—German, Dutch, and Italian, with French the working language—were made by majority vote.[23]

The decision-making jurisdiction of this nine-member body was paralleled by the Council of Ministers, which was drawn from the national governments and, though bound by High Authority decisions, could attempt to moderate its supranationalism. The Benelux countries (Belgium, the Netherlands, and Luxembourg), determined to defend the national interests of the smaller nations, had insisted on this institution during the treaty negotiations. The High Authority was further bound by the Common Assembly, consisting of seventy-eight members (eighteen each from Germany, France, and Italy; ten each from Belgium and the Netherlands; and four from Luxembourg). The assembly was designed to have control over the ECSC but was not a true legislative body. It could censure and demand the collective resignation of the High Authority (a step that was never applied). Most important, the treaty mandated a Court of Justice, the highest body of appeal, based on two principles: the rule of law and the right of appeal. Member states, enterprises, and associations had the right to appeal decisions of the High Authority to this court and have them declared void. The Court of Justice was composed of one judge per state who were charged to act independently of their governments and were appointed for a renewable term of six years. The fifth institution created by the treaty, the Consultative Committee, represented economic and social interests such as producers, workers, and consumers. To Monnet, this community, with its new institutions, was the "beginning of Europe" (Document 21).

After working six months to make the High Authority operational, the members began in 1953 to create a single common market in which coal and steel products could be sold competitively. (See Figure 2.) However, the High Authority soon discovered that their goal of creating a genuine common market in these two sectors was unrealistic. Although the Treaty of Paris had called for a five-year transitional period of two stages—first dismantling tariffs and other trade restrictions, and only then moving to establish a free common market—they discovered that national intransigence and objections made eliminating tariffs and quotas impossible. Coal and steel commerce had been regulated since the beginning of the century, and each nation's policies were dictated by national goals and vested interests. Power struggles arose not just with industry but also with governments that were reluctant to cede control to the High Authority. It was powerless to alter producer or government practices regarding steel price setting, marketing, and fuel pricing. As a result, the ECSC's cartel policy proved ineffective.[24]

Figure 2 (opposite). *Jean Monnet (left) and Robert Schuman, Luxembourg, May 9, 1953*

Pioneers Jean Monnet and Robert Schuman in Luxembourg on May 9, 1953, after discussing issues facing the European Coal and Steel Community (ECSC), the new organization created by the Schuman Plan which they jointly initiated. The strong, trusting relationship between Monnet and Schuman began in 1947 when Monnet, head of the Monnet Plan, and Schuman, the French finance minister, worked closely together to solve the difficult financial problems inherent in the reconstruction of France. (Pierre Uri is behind Monnet to the left and Walter Hallstein is behind Monnet's shoulder to the right.)

Copyright: European Commission/Pol Aschman; *Source:* Médiathèque de la Fondation Jean Monnet pour l'Europe, Lausanne, Switzerland.

The Failure of the Idea of a European Defense Community

The Six, after long negotiations, had signed a treaty creating the European Defense Community (EDC) in May 1952, and all except France had ratified it by early 1954. Britain again refused to join a supranational organization. Although the U.S. government had initially opposed the idea, by midsummer of 1951 Monnet had persuaded McCloy and General Dwight Eisenhower, NATO's supreme allied commander in Europe, of the EDC's utility as a further step toward integration and a means to foster European security (Document 24). After the French agreed to certain concessions, these two Americans became strong supporters of the revised version of the plan, which seemed to be the best way to implement German rearmament and promote further European union. American officials continued to press for a united Europe, believing it would lighten U.S. burdens and offer a solution to the problems of Soviet expansionism, German nationalism, European weakness, American isolationism, and Franco-German animosity. It also seemed to them the only way to guarantee both French security and German equality.[25]

Adenauer had initially reacted negatively to the EDC because he was convinced that French intentions were not honorable. He feared that the French solution to the problem of security with West Germany was to cooperate with the Soviet Union. He was concerned that if the four occupying powers aimed to neutralize Germany while simultaneously withdrawing their occupying troops, American involvement in Europe would be diminished. Fearing invasion from East Germany, he continued to press for a West German defense contribution and a reorganization of German relations with the Western powers as a way of keeping the United States in Europe. But once Truman approved the EDC in July 1951, Adenauer accepted it. He saw no prospect for any other solution and feared even more the consequences of not ratifying the treaty. Moreover, the United States had agreed to incorporate the German defense contribution into the framework of the EDC, abolish the rearmament ban imposed by the allies, plan for full German membership in NATO, and end allied occupation when the treaty entered into force, which would restore German sovereignty over domestic and foreign affairs.[26]

The memories of war that haunted the French and their fear of German rearmament doomed the EDC treaty from the start. The French Communists opposed it, and nationalists such as de Gaulle, out of power since 1946, denounced it as yielding French sovereignty.

Others claimed that it would be the end of France as a nation and of its cherished institutions—the army and the empire. French government leaders had signed the treaty in May 1952 with the tacit understanding that there would be no attempt to ratify it, and no French government dared to bring it to parliament. By August 1954, the new prime minister, Pierre Mendès-France, realized that the EDC was a stumbling block to launching new foreign policy initiatives. He decided to end the stalemate by calling on the National Assembly to adopt a procedural motion, and by a vote of 319 to 264, the French assembly killed the EDC[27] (Document 26).

The failure of the EDC was a defeat for integration, federalism, and supranationalism. It also revealed certain political realities. It demonstrated that French politicians could not tolerate the rearmament of Germany under the EDC's terms. French leaders also detested the idea of France being embedded in a European government. In addition, the EDC's collapse indicated the misgivings Europeans felt about sharing control in defense or foreign policy issues. Finally, it underscored their mistrust of supranational communities and left the problem of harnessing German power unresolved.[28]

Although the EDC scheme failed, Monnet's strategy of using it to satisfy the Americans and save the Schuman Plan succeeded. Simply proposing the EDC allowed the French government to pursue a strategy of moderating German economic recovery while delaying U.S. attempts to rearm Germany. Although the EDC defeat discouraged integrationists in the short term, it generated constructive thinking about possible ways to continue the process. The very existence of the ECSC, which focused on a practical, narrow goal, generated momentum to move European integration forward. It pushed European leaders to think positively about additional concrete forms of integration as a means of preventing another war.[29]

The Impact of the ECSC

The demise of the EDC was a real setback to the cause of European integration and for a while overshadowed the accomplishments of the ECSC. Even though the ECSC could not successfully create a genuine common market in coal and steel, its mere establishment as an operational international body was significant. In its first two years, the ECSC's two hundred civil servants, representing six nations, had established a functioning international organization that gathered information, issued decrees, and attempted to enforce regulations, creating a new international political framework. Decisions, taken by majority vote of the High Authority, forced member states to consult and negotiate constantly. This process facilitated compromise, occasionally inhibited unilateral action by some states, and served as a brake on nationalism in some limited ways. By instituting the principle that supranational decisions be made through majority vote, the ECSC showed that nations could share some sovereignty and proved that a structured multinational entity could deal with some common economic problems.

The ECSC demonstrated that an institution, based on the rule of law, could serve as a framework for changing patterns of thinking and behavior (Document 21). By institutionalizing cooperation, the ECSC took a step toward establishing a foundation for peace: This novel community changed the context within which the former wartime rivals thought and worked. As a result, the ECSC furthered Franco-German rapprochement and brought Europe closer to peace.[30]

While Monnet, through the ECSC, intended to impose long-term controls on the German coal and steel industry, the creation of the ECSC and subsequent negotiations had the unintended consequence of liberating German coal and steel from allied controls and restoring them to their traditionally dominant position in the Western European economy. Gradually, Germany and France came to recognize the mutual benefits of restoring Ruhr industry to private ownership. The Americans supported this development because they did not want to let the breakup of the cartels jeopardize German rearmament and because they were committed to the Ruhr restoration through new institutional arrangements. The change in attitudes inspired a new degree of confidence between France and Germany and led to more far-reaching integration.[31]

Increased Commitments to European Integration

The cold war continued to overshadow European leaders in the 1950s and motivated them to continue their efforts to collaborate. A diplomatic note from the Soviets in March 1952 proposing that the four powers conclude a peace treaty reflected Stalin's concern about West German remilitarization within the Western alliance. Although international tension subsided after Stalin's death in March 1953 and the end of the Korean War that same year, Soviet repression of Eastern Europe continued. The Soviets suppressed workers' demonstrations in East Berlin in June 1953 and squashed an opposition movement in Hungary in 1956. Moscow made overtures to Adenauer, hoping to gain German neutrality, but the chancellor feared Soviet subversion and aggression and resisted these pressures.

Adenauer welcomed an alternative to the EDC proposed by the new British prime minister, Anthony Eden. Eden suggested extending the Treaty of Brussels—signed by Britain, France, and the Benelux countries in March 1948—to include Italy and Germany. After Eden obtained the leaders' consent, they agreed to terminate the occupation of Germany, recognize West German sovereignty, and establish a new organization, the Western European Union (WEU), which included West Germany and Italy as members. This agreement, signed on October 23, 1954, is known as the Paris Accords. The WEU, directly incorporated into NATO, became the new foundation for a European defense system. West Germany thus became an ally under NATO, with its forces placed under NATO's integrated command. To reassure France, the British gave the WEU a guarantee that it had withheld from the EDC—that British troops would be stationed in West Germany unless a majority of its partners consented to their withdrawal. French prime minister Mendès-France had pressured Adenauer during the final WEU negotiations to accept the French demand that a plebiscite be held in the Saar. Faced with the threat that France would not otherwise sign the Paris Accords, the chancellor finally assented. In his press conference in Paris, Adenauer proclaimed October 23, 1954, as "the day of reconciliation with France."[32]

The three-year EDC debate transformed the American commitment to West Germany. Washington's efforts to persuade the French to adopt the EDC acclimated U.S. officials and politicians to the idea of having American troops there. They further recognized that the British and American forces in West Germany not only protected Europe against the Russians, who loomed more threatening after the Korean War, but also afforded the Europeans protection against themselves. In December 1954, the United States committed to defending the frontiers of NATO countries with its own forces. This greatly expanded the U.S. commitment to Europe and thus reassured Europeans that they would not be abandoned.[33]

The Paris Accords, with their expanded U.S. and British commitments to West Germany, helped provide increased security and stability to Europe. Reassured, Western European leaders were able to focus on ways to continue with integration. The ECSC and EDC negotiations and the Council of Europe meetings had fueled debates and generated new ideas about European unity. Some statesmen proposed further cooperation on health matters, postal service, and transport. Others proposed an agricultural common market directed by a supranational institution. Dutch foreign minister Johan Willem Beyen had announced in 1952 that sectoral integration was insufficient to promote economic development and, ultimately, political union. Beyen argued that the six nations should organize a customs union, whereby all forms of trade discrimination (such as quotas and tariffs on intracommunity trade) would be abolished and a common external tariff would be applied to all imports. Because the Netherlands depended on international trade and tariffs hindered the Dutch economy, Beyen favored regional economic integration (Document 25). In 1953, he proposed the creation of a general common market. Since shared national sovereignty over a single sector had not worked, a few officials argued that it was more logical to plan for the integration of whole economies. Some popular support for integration in general and for an initiative to counter the EDC's collapse assured politicians that they could continue to explore their options.[34]

THE ROAD TO CLOSER UNION

Many factors in late 1954 and 1955—the ECSC experiment, significant economic growth and trade liberalization, a stable political climate and increase in security, and the continuing debates about methods of international cooperation—spurred European leaders to continue to explore integration in the economic sphere. The EDC debacle also played a critical role in their search for closer union.[35] Although most leaders understood that the ECSC's supranational structure was not a viable model to imitate in 1955, the harsh rhetoric in the French National Assembly over the EDC motivated French prime minister Edgar Faure to propose countermeasures in the cultural and educational field to improve Franco-German relations. The resolution of the Saar problem—as a result of a referendum there in October 1955, in which inhabitants voted overwhelmingly to return to West Germany—further improved Franco-German relations. The Saar was smoothly reincorporated into West Germany in January 1957.

The EDC's demise also brought Belgium's foreign minister Paul-Henri Spaak and Monnet together in September 1954 to discuss ways to move integration forward. (See Figure 3.) In conversations throughout that fall, they agreed to continue their efforts to further integra-

Figure 3. *Jean Monnet and Paul-Henri Spaak (right), Strasbourg, September 10, 1952*

Jean Monnet and Paul-Henri Spaak, shown here conversing in Strasbourg, September 10, 1952, met for the first time in Washington in 1941 and discussed what would have to be done after the war to safeguard peace and Europe's future. These two pioneers, who helped promote integration in the late 1940s and early 1950s, worked as an effective team to move integration forward after the EDC debacle in 1954 and were responsible for persuading the foreign ministers of the Six to meet in Messina in June 1955.

Copyright: European Commission; *Source:* Médiathèque de la Fondation Jean Monnet pour l'Europe, Lausanne, Switzerland.

tion, deciding that Monnet would prepare the proposals and Spaak would take the diplomatic initiative. Monnet announced his retirement as president of the ECSC's High Authority in November 1954, but as both Spaak and Adenauer urged him to stay, he used their pleas as an opportunity to advance the integration process. He told them that he would remain at the High Authority until a successor was appointed if they met his condition: that the Six commit themselves to negotiate treaties on new economic communities.[36]

During the first half of 1955, Spaak, Monnet, and Beyen relaunched integration discussions by convening a series of intergovernmental meetings, including the foreign ministers of all six ECSC nations, to discuss new proposals. Beyen argued for a customs union. Spaak thought Beyen's plan too ambitious and preferred Monnet's plan for a sectoral atomic energy community. Whereas Spaak believed that economic integration would lead to political union, Beyen was more concerned with prospects for economic growth. Under pressure from Beyen, Spaak incorporated the "general" approach of Beyen with the "sectoral" approach of Monnet and encapsulated the two in what became known as the Benelux Memorandum.[37]

Monnet and his colleagues had developed a plan for a sectoral supranational community that would pool atomic energy resources for peaceful purposes. Monnet knew that nuclear energy could be a cheap source of electrical power, and he hoped to get assistance for France to develop its nuclear program, which was inferior to that of the British, Soviets, and Americans. He also hoped that involving the Germans in this endeavor would help constrain them. The "peaceful atom," Monnet claimed, would unify Europe[38] (Document 30).

Released in May 1955, the Benelux Memorandum generated much debate in the business and political circles of the six nations. Various forms of regional economic integration, including a customs union and a common market, were widely discussed. In West Germany, the debate focused on how to liberalize trade. Economics minister Ludwig Erhard viewed a customs union as protectionist and, fearing that regional arrangements would hinder global free trade, advocated a multilateral approach. Walter Hallstein, a foreign ministry official, advocated a customs union for both political and economic reasons. Adenauer sided with Hallstein and also supported the atomic energy proposal as a result of pressure from Monnet. In deeply protectionist France, the business and political elites wanted to use Monnet's atomic energy community to gain access to European resources for their civilian and military atomic energy programs. Their nationalistic motivations were transparent to other members of the Six. Economist Robert Marjolin was one of France's few proponents of economic liberalization; he believed that the French economy could realize its full potential only through membership in a common market. Since Spaak and Monnet linked the sectoral atomic energy plan with Beyen's common market and customs union proposals, the discussions continued.[39]

At their meeting in Messina, Italy, in early June 1955, the foreign ministers of the Six approved the French government's choice of René

Mayer, former French prime minister, to succeed Monnet as president of the High Authority. Their discussion then focused on new European communities. They proceeded slowly; Franco-German distrust was still strong, despite the marked improvement in their relations. Luxembourg premier Joseph Bech, who was committed to integration and chaired the meetings, joined Spaak and Beyen as the driving forces in these complex and delicate negotiations. At the last minute, the ministers agreed to establish an intergovernmental committee, including representatives from each of the Six and headed by Spaak, to continue discussions on the atomic energy and common market proposals and report back to the foreign ministers. Repeating much of the Benelux Memorandum, the Messina Declaration called for pooling information and work on the uses of nuclear energy, as well as for the establishment of a customs union that would lead to a common market. By insisting on a sectoral nuclear energy community, the foreign ministers gave the Europeanists in the French government a chance to be involved in the process. The Messina gathering kept the idea of an integrated Europe alive and all the options open while the governments of the Six awaited concrete proposals from Spaak's committee[40] (Document 27).

After Messina, the sixty-six-year-old Monnet, no longer president of the High Authority, worked to publicize the idea of a united Europe (Document 28). He formed an international committee of political party and trade union leaders to pressure national governments to further integration, winning enthusiastic support from three German and other ECSC trade unions and from French socialists. On October 13, 1955, Monnet announced the establishment of the Action Committee for the United States of Europe, a lobby for integration in the six ECSC countries (Document 29). Under the skilled leadership of the wise, intellectual Dutch foreign ministry official Max Kohnstamm, the Action Committee's secretary-general, the committee became an effective network of politicians, civil servants, and labor leaders working together to advance integration. At its first session, on January 18, 1956, the Action Committee adopted a resolution supporting the idea of a European atomic energy community, called Euratom, for civilian and peaceful purposes (Document 30). Through the committee's efforts, resolutions in favor of Euratom were introduced in each legislature of the Six, except Italy's, during the spring and summer of 1956. Euratom also received strong endorsement from Washington[41] (Document 32).

On May 29–30, 1956, the foreign ministers of the Six met in Venice to consider the report drawn up by Spaak's committee. Written largely by Monnet's brilliant, eccentric friend Pierre Uri, German high official Hans von der Groeben, and Belgian diplomat Albert Hupperts, the Spaak Report proposed the creation of two new communities. One would be a free trade community modeled on the Beyen Plan, with the gradual reduction of tariffs over time. The second would be a sectoral community to pool atomic energy for peaceful purposes: Euratom. Spaak recalled that his committee had faced two alternatives: "We could establish a simple customs union or a common market. We decided to go for the bolder of the two."[42] The Spaak Report focused mainly on proposing a common market with a customs union as its nucleus, around which the market could be created. Leaders and popular opinion in five of the six countries favored the common market. The Benelux nations welcomed the increased trade and economic benefits a common market would bring. The Italians passionately supported the initiative because closer European unity would bring them economic benefits, increase their international stature and voice, and nourish greater solidarity between Italian and German Catholics and Christian Democrats. France's strong protectionist tradition meant that French opinion opposed the common market, though it supported Euratom. The French insisted at Venice that any final agreement must include access to the common market for the products from their colonies. Since France would not proceed with the common market negotiations without Euratom and Germany would not continue without the common market, Spaak proposed, and the Six agreed, to charge his intergovernmental committee with drafting treaties on both proposals. The decision demonstrated that the Six agreed in principle with the Spaak Report.[43]

Negotiating the Treaties of Rome

The difficult intergovernmental conference negotiations in Brussels that produced the Treaties of Rome began in the summer of 1956. At times, discussions came to a halt, and differences seemed irreconcilable. But memories of the war and fear of the consequences of failing to reach an agreement motivated the participants to continue. Spaak was an energetic chairman; his negotiating skill, political dynamism, and ability to pressure individual delegations played a decisive role in the talks. He called in prime ministers and foreign ministers, parliamentarians and interest groups, to meet with the delegations from the Six and advance the process. The fear of trade liberalization in protectionist France remained the main stumbling block. Assisted by Foreign Minister Christian Pineau, Secretary of State for Foreign Affairs Maurice Faure, and Robert Marjolin, his key adviser, Prime Minister Guy Mollet's strategy was to win as many concessions as possible from the other leaders while appeasing officials in Paris when they were denied (Document 33). The other five countries gave in to many of the French demands because they knew French domestic support was fragile and there could be no viable common market without France.[44]

Adenauer directed his cabinet to strongly support European integration because he believed that it was critical for his nation's and Europe's future (Document 31). He had won the support of the Social Democrats, who believed as he did that the proposed common market offered his nation an outlet for its booming economy, and most West Germans supported his European policy. He knew he had to cooperate with France in the negotiations for political reasons and enjoyed being on an equal footing with the French. But his willingness to subordinate some economic objectives to strategic considerations annoyed colleagues who resented his deference to France. One of the most contentious battles occurred when the Germans opposed the French demand that its overseas territories be associated with the common market. Mollet and Adenauer finally agreed to give preferential treatment to the overseas territories and to establish a special, separate fund for development assistance, with Germany as the largest contributor. With regard to the Spaak Report's recommendation that the customs union be implemented in three stages over twelve years, these two leaders agreed that a nation could delay by two years its implementation, but after that time, arbitration would be required. Thus a nation could not prevent outright the implementation of the customs union. Other disputes over attempts to equalize pay and social systems were settled by all six members.[45]

Amid great fanfare, on March 25, 1957, the heads of state of the six ECSC countries signed two treaties of economic union in Rome collectively called the Treaty of Rome.[46] (See Map 2.) The first treaty created a common market, the European Economic Community (EEC). The second created the European Atomic Energy Community, or Euratom. As Spaak wrote, "It was an unforgettable ceremony, which the Italians had organized in the grand manner. . . . The bells of Rome rang out to salute the birth of the new Europe." He called it the first stage of "a political revolution" (Document 34). Pineau, arguing that the Six were not an exclusive club, expressed his hope that other

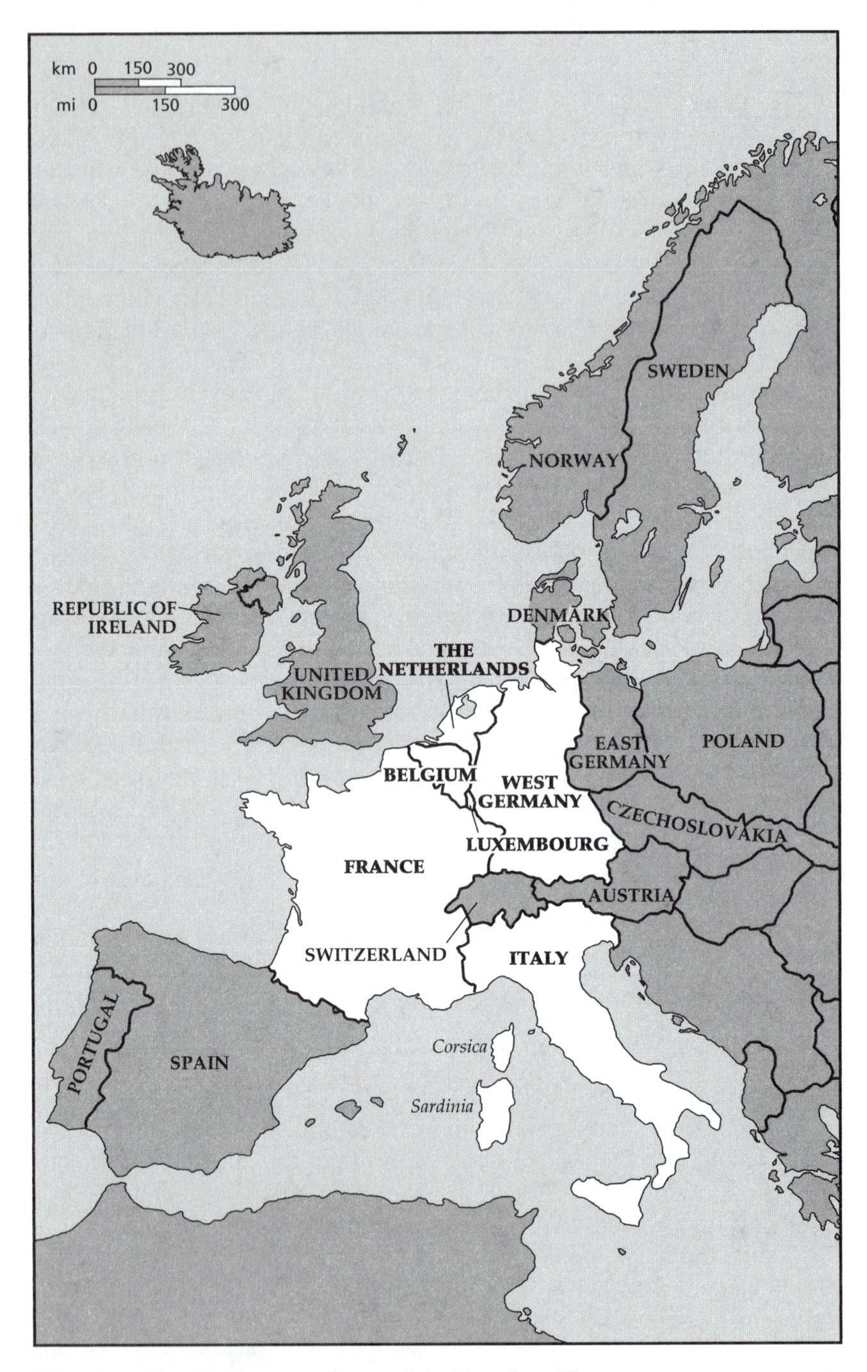

Map 2. *The Six Signatory States of the Treaties of Rome*

Six nations—France, West Germany, Italy, Belgium, the Netherlands, and Luxembourg—signed the Treaties of Rome on March 25, 1957.

Source: Lucinda Brown.

countries, including Britain, would join. Hallstein stated, "We are not integrating economies, we are integrating politics. We are not just sharing our furniture, we are jointly building a new and bigger house."[47]

The preambles to the EEC and Euratom treaties reflect the founders' vision "to lay the foundations of an ever closer union among the peoples of Europe" through economic integration and to create a climate in which peace could flourish. The EEC treaty stated that European nations were "resolved by thus pooling their resources to preserve and strengthen peace and liberty." The Euratom treaty stated that the nuclear energy industry "will permit the advancement of the cause of peace." Its main objectives were the promotion of research and the peaceful uses of nuclear energy; the dissemination of information; the protection of health and safety; the equitable distribution of ores and nuclear fuels; the supervision of nuclear materials; the facilitation of investment in the industry; and the establishment of a common market in specialized materials, capital, employment, and equipment.[48]

The European Economic Community

The EEC treaty, the most important of the two and often called the Rome Treaty or Treaty of Rome, established both a customs union and a common market. Since creating a common market was not immediately politically feasible, it was expressed as an aspiration. This took the form of a statement of goals and an outline of the essential principles of a common market, such as the free movement of persons, services, and capital. The treaty also called for a common commercial policy, a common transport policy, a competition policy, limited monetary policy cooperation, and the coordination of macroeconomic policy, and it included various other community policies and principles, vaguely expressed. In contrast, the provisions in the treaty for a customs union were quite specific: to abolish all quantitative restrictions on internal trade, establish a common external tariff, and adhere to a twelve-year timetable for implementing this ambitious program of economic liberalization. The treaty stated the leaders' goal to create a common agricultural policy but gave no indication of when that would be achieved. It also called for the creation of the European Social Fund to retrain and assist workers and established the European Investment Bank to provide inexpensive loans for regional development and other projects.[49] The EEC was popularly known as "the Common Market" in the press, political speeches, and policy announcements, even though a common market remained merely an aspiration until the late 1980s and 1990s.

The institutions created by the EEC treaty reflect the ingenuity of the pioneers of European union. The innovative governing structure they designed enabled their new organization to function and endure. No other international organization like it existed. The creators modeled EEC institutions on the ECSC and the Council of Europe, but they modified and improved them to be more workable. The new EEC Council of Ministers, the decision-making intergovernmental body representing the national governments, adopted the High Authority's use of weighted voting, which based votes on a nation's population. Out of a total of seventeen votes, the larger countries—France, Germany, and Italy—each had four votes, the Netherlands and Belgium each had two votes, and Luxembourg had one. Sensitive to feelings about national sovereignty, the drafters of the EEC treaty agreed that the decisions and actions of the Council of Ministers would be taken by unanimity, simple majority, or qualified majority voting, depending on the importance of the issue.[50]

The EEC treaty also created a new institution, the European Commission, a supranational body made up of nine individuals appointed by each member government. These commissioners became international civil servants and remained independent of their governments. France, Germany, and Italy were each entitled to two commissioners, the other states to one each. This body was charged with administering the treaty and community law, initiating and implementing community legislation and regulations, recommending policies, and acting as a brake on nationalism. In addition, the treaty created a parliament of 142 representatives, with the number from each nation based on the size of its population. This parliament could censure the Commission, but it was primarily an advisory body. The Court of Justice was made up of seven judges, one from each nation plus one appointed by the Council of Ministers. Appointed for renewable six-year terms, the judges were interpreters of the treaties. As in the ECSC, this court enforced decisions and was the final court of appeal. It handled all disputes arising from the three communities—ECSC, EEC, and Euratom—or between members. The EEC treaty also stated that member states could extend economic integration to sectors not mentioned in the treaty if the other members voted unanimously to agree.[51]

The leaders of the Six pushed for the rapid ratification of the treaties by each government. France's prime minister placed the treaties before the National Assembly a week after they were signed.

The French debate centered on fears of German domination, mass migration, and job loss, whereas in Germany the opposition focused on arguments that German products needed trade protection. The influential network of Monnet's Action Committee helped ensure ratification because it effectively lobbied the legislators of the Six. Once France and Germany had ratified the treaties, the other nations followed. All ratifications were completed by the end of 1957, and the ECC was launched on January 1, 1958.

The pioneers of European integration brought their six Western European nations together in a voluntary economic union in 1957 and thereby established a foundation for lasting peace. These pioneering leaders—the heads of state and principal statesmen, foreign ministers, diplomats, civil servants, heads of organizations and committees, and other influential individuals among their elites—demonstrated political leadership, vision, ingenuity, pragmatism, entrepreneurship in policymaking and persistence in their pursuit of a closer union. Whether they were among the victors or the defeated powers, the scars of war and memories of the physical destruction, human losses, and suffering motivated them to experiment with various communities and associations that encouraged collaboration. These national leaders—especially Schuman, Monnet, Adenauer, Spaak, Beyen, Bech, Mollet, and De Gasperi—as well as those who worked for a closer union—Spinelli, Marjolin, Uri, Hirsch, Hallstein, Kohnstamm, Pleven, von der Groeben, Hupperts, Pineau, Maurice Faure, and others, including members of the ECSC's High Authority—decided to take political risks and make tough decisions in the face of strong opposition in their countries. They learned from their mistakes, compromised on important issues of national interest, and continued to try to work together despite grave differences. Incrementally, between 1945 and 1957, these men discovered that they could reach some agreements on matters of mutual concern and pursue some national interests through supranational institutions. The ECSC had demonstrated that institutionalized cooperation had some success in two sectors. Therefore, they pursued more comprehensive economic integration and eventually signed the Treaties of Rome because these agreements served their national interests: furthering peace by increasing Franco-German collaboration, promoting economic growth, and strengthening Europe by uniting it. As Mark Gilbert has argued, the greatness of this postwar generation of European leaders in the first decade after 1945 was that they were "loyal both to the interests of their individual nations and to the principle of European cooperation."[52] Never before had the long-warring European nation-states united without the threat of force or coercion and agreed to limit but not eliminate each nation's sovereignty in economic matters. As Marjolin wrote, "I do not believe it is an exaggeration to say that this date [March 25, 1957] represents one of the greatest moments in Europe's history.[53]

The EEC demonstrated its success earlier than expected because the leaders of the Six implemented the clauses of the treaty on schedule. The new French president Charles de Gaulle worked with Adenauer through the Council of Ministers to help the organization achieve some of its early goals. Negotiations to establish a customs union with a common external tariff proceeded smoothly in the 1960s, and the first series of internal and external tariff measures were implemented without much dispute. The choice of the West German Walter Hallstein as the first Commission president demonstrated the extent to which Franco-German rapprochement had progressed.[54] The Council of Ministers, with a Belgian as president, established the Committee of Permanent Representatives to remain in Brussels and carry out the Council's mandates. With the appointment of judges, the Court of Justice began its work to ensure that the member states and the institutions fulfilled their treaty obligations. The parliament chose Robert Schuman as president and hailed the new era of international cooperation.[55]

De Gaulle and the EEC

Between 1958 and 1963, the EEC was dominated by the policies of the ambitious French president, Charles de Gaulle. His compelling goals were to restore France's international prestige and to enhance his influence in the EEC. Although many feared that he would hinder the EEC because of his earlier opposition to both it and Euratom, de Gaulle fully implemented the clauses of the Rome Treaty because he believed that the EEC would help revitalize the French economy.[56] De Gaulle implemented domestic financial reforms that helped the French economy maximize the benefits of the customs union. The exposure of the French economy to foreign competition stimulated industrial production and modernization.

The British had displayed little interest in the 1955 Messina talks on integration or in the Rome Treaty negotiations. They preferred a limited intergovernmental free trade area, and wished to preserve preferential trade with their Commonwealth countries. When, after the treaty was signed, the British proposed a free trade area to include the EEC as a bloc, the EEC leaders rejected the scheme. British prime minister Harold Macmillan countered this rebuff by creating, in January 1960, a rival trading bloc, the European Free Trade Association (EFTA), with six other non-EEC Western European nations: Austria, Denmark, Norway, Portugal, Sweden, and Switzerland. The United States stood with the Germans and French in opposition to EFTA. Publicly, the U.S. administration continued to argue that the EEC's liberal trade policy, along with the ongoing negotiations for an international trade organization, were the best solutions for transatlantic and intra-European trade. Privately, the United States disliked the tariffs erected by the EEC, which discriminated against U.S. goods.[57]

De Gaulle attempted to create international structures outside the EEC and NATO to increase his international influence. But his proposals in September 1958—including that the United States and Britain share their atomic information with France and agree to consult him on the use of nuclear weapons should war arise—were rejected as both undercutting NATO and being alienating to the Germans. Then, in November 1961, de Gaulle proposed the Fouchet Plan, an intergovernmental organization for foreign and security cooperation (Document 35). The EEC's leaders opposed the plan, seeing it as a ploy both to increase his personal power and prevent the EEC from acquiring too much influence over national governments. That scheme, too, collapsed.

The British Application to Join the EEC

The early success of the EEC generated a flurry of applications from nations seeking to join. Israel, Greece, and Turkey were the first to apply, in 1958 and 1959, and Denmark, Ireland, Norway, and Britain followed in 1961. In spite of EFTA's progress, it had not countered the growing importance of the EEC, and the EFTA countries were still trading more with the EEC than with each other. Britain wanted to preserve its trade with the EEC because it needed a market larger than EFTA. Its economic performance, which lagged behind that of its European competitors, and its diminished role and influence in world politics, as well as the Commonwealth's declining percentage of British trade, convinced Macmillan to reverse his earlier opposition to the EEC (Document 37). Negotiations to join the EEC began in the spring of 1962 and were nearly completed by the end of that year.[58]

Britain's application strained relations between Bonn, Paris, and Washington. Adenauer disliked Macmillan personally, but he favored

British membership in the EEC, at least initially, because he believed that access to Britain's market would benefit Germany as well as the EEC. He also recognized the usefulness of siding with Washington (which supported the British application), not only because of Germany's dependence on the United States for security but also to calm the German critics who feared he was getting too close to de Gaulle. By the summer of 1962, however, Adenauer had changed his mind and become convinced that Britain should not be admitted to the EEC.

The United States supported British membership in the EEC, believing it would benefit the EEC economically and politically and thereby strengthen European unity and Western Europe as a bulwark against the Soviet Union. Tensions with Moscow had greatly increased because of the Berlin crises between 1958 and 1961, where Soviet and East German probes tested Western resolve in the western section of Berlin. These challenges culminated in the construction of the Berlin Wall in 1961. Washington officials saw mainly long-range economic benefits to the American economy from British membership, but they also hoped that Britain would take a leadership role in liberalizing European trade. In addition, President John F. Kennedy saw Britain as an important element in his "Grand Design," his plan for a new transatlantic partnership that would enhance American hegemony (Document 36).

In a dramatic display of his power, de Gaulle vetoed Britain's application for EEC membership at a press conference in January 1963 (Document 38). The French president wanted to assert his dominance in Europe, and he feared that a British challenge risked French leadership in the EEC, which rested on the Franco-German axis. De Gaulle had fought energetically since coming to power for the protectionist common agricultural policy (CAP) in the EEC (as stipulated in the Rome Treaty; see glossary), and he had been irritated by Britain's attempts, during negotiations, to get preferential treatment for Commonwealth agricultural products. He wanted guaranteed access to EEC markets that would protect highly subsidized French agriculture from cheaper, non-EEC imports. Because French agriculture was so productive, he needed to export the surplus, but such subsidized products were not internationally competitive. The CAP gave him both an EEC-wide market with guaranteed high prices and subsidies for exports to countries outside the EEC, with the cost shared by all EEC members. Both Germany and the United States opposed the CAP: Germany did not grow enough food and relied on imports, and the

United States, which produced cheaper food products, did not want to be excluded from the German or other EEC markets. Lengthy battles between the French and the Germans resulted by the end of 1962 in a victory for de Gaulle: the CAP would be established. But de Gaulle feared that Britain, with its very different agricultural interests and political power, would sabotage the CAP arrangement he had negotiated with great difficulty with the Commission, Germany, and other EEC partners.[59]

De Gaulle also strongly opposed strengthening the Atlantic partnership advocated by the Kennedy administration in its Grand Design. De Gaulle viewed the special relationship between the United States and Britain, along with Britain's proposed entry into the EEC, as strengthening America's role in Europe. The Kennedy-Macmillan deal, in December 1962, to provide Britain with U.S. Polaris missiles (known as the Nassau Accords) had further convinced de Gaulle that Britain was subservient to the United States. The French president did not want a Europe dominated by the Americans; by rejecting Britain, he demonstrated that he could deliver a simultaneous blow to Washington. De Gaulle's veto represented an insult to the British, a setback for Kennedy's Grand Design, and a challenge to American supremacy in NATO.[60]

A week after vetoing Britain's application to the EEC, the French president dealt another blow to Washington by signing with Adenauer the Treaty of Friendship and Reconciliation (Document 39). Adenauer had developed a close relationship with de Gaulle since 1958, accepting invitations to de Gaulle's country home and responding to the general's efforts to cultivate their relationship. Adenauer believed that solid relations with France were critical to the success of European integration, which he knew was also in West Germany's national interest, and key to reestablishing Germany's international standing and Western European stability. As Adenauer's biographer Hans-Peter Schwarz remarked, by 1961 the chancellor "was under the spell of the tall General." Both nations, under the Elysée Treaty, as it was known, pledged to consult each other on foreign policy decisions, hold biannual summits, and develop an active youth exchange program.[61]

The treaty alarmed many people in West Germany, including members of Adenauer's own Christian Democratic Union party, who disliked de Gaulle's anti-American and anti-EEC policies and feared that Adenauer was overly influenced by him. As a result, the West German parliament added a preamble to the treaty, asserting that West Germany's primary commitment to existing alliance obligations was not subordinated to the Franco-German entente: Germany remained committed to its multilateral obligations. This parliamentary action, which humiliated Adenauer, led to his resignation later in 1963. Though weakened, the Elysée Treaty was the culminating symbol of Franco-German cooperation, the cornerstone of a new integrated Europe.[62]

De Gaulle's policies toward the EEC in 1962 and early 1963 exacerbated France's fractious relations with Britain and the United States, and his carefully crafted CAP agreement provoked anger in Washington. Although American farmers grumbled loudly about high discriminatory EEC tariffs, political, strategic, and economic interests dictated that the United States support further European integration by acquiescing in the EEC's common agricultural policy. President Kennedy declared, "We have to live with de Gaulle" (Document 40). As Secretary of State Dean Rusk wrote American ambassadors in Europe, U.S. foreign policy "is guided by judgment that in a fundamental sense security and progress of Western Europe and United States are indivisible. . . . Neither area can go it alone without imperiling the survival and progress of both."[63] Despite his efforts to create international structures outside the EEC and NATO, de Gaulle helped ensure that the process of European integration would continue.

Although de Gaulle implemented the EEC treaty's clauses faithfully, his hostility to supranationalism and his pursuit of an independent nuclear weapons policy doomed Euratom from the start. In 1962, the French president replaced Etienne Hirsch, Euratom's president, with his own minister of the interior to ensure Euratom's demise. As de Gaulle explained, "We are no longer in the era when Monsieur Monnet gave orders."[64] De Gaulle viewed his nationalist nuclear policy and the development of his *force de frappe* (nuclear strike force) as an instrument of political independence, and he refused to tolerate restrictions on military weapons development.[65] Moreover, Euratom faced opposition from private industry and from the other governments, such as Italy and Germany, that promoted the growth of their own national nuclear power programs. At the same time, the need for nuclear power diminished, thanks to an overabundance of coal and the resulting drop in its price, as well as new oil discoveries in the Middle East. Not viewed as an important organization that furthered the national interests of the Six, Euratom was merged institutionally with the EEC and ECSC in 1967 and marginalized. It functioned as a center for the dissemination of information on nuclear energy research and related issues.

Along with Adenauer's and de Gaulle's efforts, favorable economic and political circumstances contributed to the initial accomplishments of the EEC. Western Europe experienced an economic boom in the late 1950s and early 1960s, making many Europeans feel that the future was bright. Politically, détente seemed close at hand after the 1955 Geneva Summit between the three Western powers (the United States, Britain, and France) and the Soviet Union, the first meeting of these cold war enemies since the war. The summit leaders signed a treaty recognizing Austria's neutrality and removed all occupying forces. This optimistic climate made it easier for national governments to implement the Rome Treaty. Although de Gaulle's policy of grandeur irritated Washington and London, the Kennedy administration continued to pursue its Grand Design to strengthen the Atlantic partnership, acquiesce in the CAP, and strongly support integration. And although the new Franco-German treaty angered some in Paris, Bonn, London, and Washington, it was a critical step in the incremental process of European integration set in motion by its pioneers after 1945, and it helped ensure that this process would continue (Document 42).

"Ever Closer Union":[66] The EEC to the EU, 1963–2006

The EEC, the new organization established by the pioneers of European integration, limited but did not eliminate each member state's sovereignty. Known as the European Union (EU) since 1992, it has become "a regional organization unlike any other," wrote Desmond Dinan, "with unprecedented economic and political authority."[67] Andrew Moravcsik has argued that the EU "remains the most successful experiment in political institution building since World War II."[68] It has evolved into a "unique form of confederalism," Mark Gilbert has asserted, and is "an international mechanism that has been gradually assembled by its member states to manage, extend and further economic cooperation between Europe's states."[69] Institutionally hybrid in nature because it combines both intergovernmental and federalist elements, the EU does not fit any textbook pattern or political scientist's paradigm. In 2005, the EU's ambassador to the United States, former Irish prime minister John Bruton, described it as "the world's only multinational, voluntary democratic space where people have democratically and collectively agreed to work together. They have made decisions about their future that go beyond the borders of a member state."[70]

From 1963 to 2006, the EEC, and subsequently the European Community (EC)[71] and then the EU, has evolved into a stable, legitimate regional organization that has made war among its member states unthinkable. Widely recognized as an influential international actor, the EU has brought national and ethnic reconciliation, democratic reform, and economic revitalization throughout the continent.[72] The EU has succeeded because national politicians, businesspeople, officials, and other key actors have responded rationally, on the whole, to changing political, economic, and strategic circumstances and have pursued pragmatic, incremental reform. As a result, they have deepened economic integration, established monetary union and a single currency, reformed and strengthened EU institutions, and added nineteen new members. In the process, the EU has become an important player on the global scene.[73]

External crises, strategic concerns, and domestic priorities motivated its leaders gradually to increase economic integration after 1963. The EC moved ahead economically in the 1960s, consolidating the common market by completing the customs union ahead of schedule in 1968, and began to act as a bloc in trade negotiations. In the 1970s, national governments agreed to fund the CAP through the EC's central budget. Buffeted by the worldwide depression, inflation, and high energy prices following OPEC's oil embargo in the wake of the 1973 Arab-Israeli war, the EC failed to eradicate nontariff barriers and promote monetary union. Nevertheless, by the late 1970s, national governments established the European Monetary System to reduce exchange rate fluctuations, and in 1984 they resolved a bitter budget dispute. Fierce economic competition as a result of incipient globalization and rapid technological change in the 1980s convinced the three main national leaders—West German chancellor Helmut Kohl, British prime minister Margaret Thatcher, and French president François Mitterrand—and the powerful Commission president Jacques Delors of the need to accelerate integration, through institutional reform, in order to revitalize European integration and make the EC more competitive. Their efforts bore fruit in the Single European Act (SEA) of 1987, which called for completion of the single market—the free movement of people, capital, services, and goods (the Rome Treaty's original goal)—by 1992. Crucially, the SEA restricted the use of the veto in the Council of Ministers to facilitate implementation of the single market.[74]

Responding to crises of governance and the need to accommodate a larger membership, national leaders agreed to incremental, pragmatic reform of the EC's institutions as economic integration progressed. Having failed to alter its institutional framework, de Gaulle provoked the "empty chair" crisis in 1965 when he withdrew French representation in the Council of Ministers. By doing so, he hoped to restrict the use of qualified majority voting, which had been mandated by the Rome Treaty. The resulting Luxembourg Compromise of 1966, which allowed member states to prevent voting in the Council of Ministers by invoking a vital national interest, was a setback for supranational decision making in the EC. In a further move toward greater intergovernmentalism, national leaders responded to the economic crises of the 1970s by establishing another institution, the European Council—comprising heads of state or government plus the Commission president—to provide strategic direction for the organization. The European Parliament, battling for greater institutional influence and budgetary powers, succeeded in gaining the direct election of its members in 1979.[75]

Over the years, EC leaders have admitted nineteen new members for political, economic, and strategic reasons. After de Gaulle left office in 1969, Britain, Ireland, and Denmark were permitted to join in 1973. In a referendum, Norwegians voted against membership. Hoping to encourage democracy in nations that had shed authoritarian governments, the EC admitted Greece in 1981 and Portugal and Spain in 1986. New members proved difficult to integrate, but enlargement continued. Austria, Finland, and Sweden joined the EU in 1995, largely because they wanted to profit from the single market's success. And in 2004, ten smaller countries became members: Cyprus, Czech Republic, Estonia, Hungary, Latvia, Lithuania, Malta, Poland, Slovakia, and Slovenia.

The fall of the Berlin Wall in 1989, and the end of Soviet occupation of Eastern Europe, raised serious security concerns for the EC. European unity and the EC's social market economy had helped contain communism and diminish its attraction. The EC's social and economic policies—a strong welfare system and protective social policies for workers—influenced Soviet President Mikhail Gorbachev's decision to pursue limited economic and social reform. But his Communist government and the Soviet Union collapsed in 1991. The resulting threat of instability in the former Soviet Union and in central and Eastern Europe, and the imminent emergence of a reunited Germany, motivated EC leaders to strengthen their economic ties and increase their political cooperation. After contentious negotiations, the twelve member states signed the Maastricht Treaty, or the Treaty on European Union (TEU), in 1992. Its key provisions called for the phased implementation of the Economic and Monetary Union (EMU), with the goal of creating a single currency in 1999, a requirement deemed necessary to ensure the success of the single market. The Maastricht Treaty established an important precedent: it allowed member states, such as Britain and Denmark, to opt out of the EMU and other provisions without jeopardizing their EU membership. The treaty also called for a common foreign and security policy to coordinate EU views and to exercise greater collective influence on unfolding events in central and Eastern Europe and a disintegrating Yugoslavia.

Strong American support for European integration continued throughout these years. The United States and the EC worked together throughout the cold war because they shared ideological values and security needs. The NATO alliance, backed by America's airpower and nuclear arsenal, shielded Western Europe from Soviet aggression and permitted integration to progress. But Jean Monnet's hope for a Europe that could treat on equal terms with the United States, embodied in the Atlantic partnership declarations, never materialized. De Gaulle's view of a political Europe able to hold its own with the United States—to be a "third force" between the United States and the Soviet Union—also remained an unrealistic dream. Periods of strain punctuated the relationship. U.S.-EC disputes in economic and foreign policy in the 1970s manifested themselves in trade conflicts over steel and agricultural exports and policy disagreements over the 1973 Arab-Israeli war. In the 1980s, transatlantic disagreement centered largely on the Reagan administration's negative view of the Soviet Union as an evil empire, the imposition of martial law in Poland, the Soviet invasion of Afghanistan, and the deployment of intermediate range nuclear missiles in Europe.

Since the end of the cold war in 1989, Europeans have felt freer to pursue independent policies. In the 1990s, the EU's weakness—evidenced by its inaction in the Balkan wars and disagreement with the United States over Kosovo—caused friction with America. But the 2003 U.S.-led invasion of Iraq to topple Saddam Hussein triggered the most serious transatlantic crisis in a generation. Although the leaders of Spain, Britain, Italy, Poland, and several other member states supported U.S. president George W. Bush, the leaders of France and Germany—supported by public opinion throughout the EU—strongly opposed the war. The Iraq crisis brought into sharp focus many U.S.-European disagreements over the legality of preventive war, the use of the death penalty, the commitment to global ecology, and the advantages of a free market economy versus a European social market economy.[76]

In 2006, at the time of this writing, the EU was deadlocked over issues of governance. Given the accession of ten new member states in 2004, the decision-making structure and voting rules established by the Treaty of Nice (2001) needed to be modified to allow the greatly enlarged EU to function effectively. Anticipating further expansion into southeastern Europe and the possible accession of Turkey, EU leaders established the Convention on the Future of Europe to craft a more efficient form of governance. Delegates from all twenty-five member states, plus Turkey, drafted the Constitutional Treaty, which consolidated the existing treaties and introduced important reforms. These included a five-year term for an EU president, a foreign minister and diplomatic service, and streamlined decision-making procedures. Approved in 2004, this complex treaty had to be ratified by all member states before it could go into effect. In 2005, first France and then the Netherlands voted down the treaty in popular referenda. To date, only fourteen states have ratified it—two by referendum, the others by a vote of their national parliaments. Consequently, the EU remains in a period of reflection and debate about how best to win approval from all its members for more workable institutional mechanisms to strengthen economic and political integration.

NOTES

[1]Walter Lipgens, *A History of European Integration* (Oxford: Clarendon Press, 1982), 1:18–35; Derek Urwin, *The Community of Europe* (London: Longman, 1991), 1–4.

[2]Desmond Dinan, *Europe Recast: A History of European Integration* (Boulder, Colo.: Lynne Rienner Publishers, 2004), 1–5.

[3]John Lewis Gaddis, *The Cold War: A New History* (New York: Penguin Press, 2005), 5–34.

[4]Dinan, *Europe Recast,* 13–19.

[5]John L. Gaddis, *We Now Know: Rethinking Cold War History* (Oxford: Clarendon Press, 1997), 1–53, 113–29; Charles S. Maier, "The Politics of Productivity: Foundations of American International Economic Policy after World War II," in *The Cold War in Europe: End of a Divided Continent,* ed. Charles S. Maier, 3rd ed. (New York: Markus Wiener, 1996), 169–201; Robert Pollard, *Economic Security and the Origins of the Cold War, 1945–1950* (New York: Columbia University Press, 1985), 33–132.

[6]Gaddis, *Cold War,* 30–32.

[7]Michael Hogan, *The Marshall Plan: America, Britain, and the Reconstruction of Western Europe, 1947–1952* (Cambridge: Cambridge University Press, 1987), 18–134; Gérard Bossuat, *L'Europe occidentale a l'heure Americaine, 1945–52* (Paris: Editions Complexe, 1992); Gérard Bossuat, *L'aide americaine et la construction européene, 1944–1954,* 2 vols. (Paris: Comité pour l'Histoire économique et financière de la France, 1992).

[8]Mark Gilbert, *Surpassing Realism: The Politics of European Integration since 1945* (Lanham, Md.: Rowman & Littlefield, 2003), 15–25.

[9]François Duchêne, *Monnet: The First Statesman of Interdependence* (New York: W. W. Norton, 1994), 152–66; Richard F. Kuisel, *Capitalism and the State in Modern France* (Cambridge: Cambridge University Press, 1981), 219–47.

[10]John Gillingham, *Coal, Steel, and the Rebirth of Europe, 1945–1955* (Cambridge: Cambridge University Press, 1991), 137–227.

[11]Duchêne, *Monnet*, 162–66; author's interview with Richard Kuisel, September 23, 2001.

[12]Duchêne, *Monnet*; William Hitchcock, *France Restored: Cold War Diplomacy and the Quest for Leadership in Europe, 1944–1954* (Chapel Hill: University of North Carolina Press, 1998), 203–6.

[13]Gilbert, *Surpassing Realism*, 28–34.

[14]Ibid., 25–31; Paul-Henri Spaak, *The Continuing Battle: Memoirs of a European, 1936–1966* (Boston: Little, Brown, 1971), 199–218.

[15]David P. Calleo, "American Power in a New World Economy," in *Economics and World Power*, ed. William H. Becker and Samuel F. Wells Jr. (New York: Columbia University Press, 1984), 391–457; Dinan, *Europe Recast*, 35–36.

[16]Jean-Pierre Rioux, *The Fourth Republic, 1944–1958* (Cambridge: Cambridge University Press, 1987), 142–45; Duchêne, *Monnet*, 182–90.

[17]Jean Monnet, *Memoirs* (Garden City, N.Y.: Doubleday, 1978), 274–93.

[18]Hans-Peter Schwarz, *Konrad Adenauer*, vol. I (Providence: Berghahn Books, 1995), 1:503–8; Duchêne, *Monnet*, 202–7.

[19]Konrad Adenauer, *Memoirs, 1945–53* (Chicago: Henry Regnery, 1966), 329–31, 375; Thomas A. Schwartz, *America's Germany* (Cambridge, Mass.: Harvard University Press, 1991), 80–217.

[20]Duchêne, *Monnet*, 227; Rioux, *Fourth Republic*, 155; Schwarz, *Adenauer*, vol. 1, 516–51.

[21]Duchêne, *Monnet*, 207–29; Monnet, *Memoirs*, 345–50; Thomas Schwartz, "The Transnational Partnership: Jean Monnet and Jack McCloy," in *Monnet and the Americans*, ed. Clifford P. Hackett (Washington, D.C.: Jean Monnet Council, 1995), 184–88; Irwin Wall, *The United States and the Making of Postwar France, 1945–1954* (Cambridge: Cambridge University Press, 1991), 189–220.

[22]Dinan, *Europe Recast*, 46–55; Edmund Dell, *The Schuman Plan and the British Abdication of Leadership in Europe* (Oxford: Oxford University Press, 1995).

[23]Dirk Spiereburg and Raymond Poidevin, *The History of the High Authority of the European Coal and Steel Community* (London: Weidenfeld and Nicolson, 1994), 43–78; Duchêne, *Monnet*, 235–36.

[24]Gillingham, *Coal*, 319–42.

[25]Duchêne, *Monnet*, 231–33; Monnet, *Memoirs*, 358–60; Schwartz, "Transnational," 189–90; Schwarz, *Adenauer*, vol. 1, 622–23; Ernest R. May, "The American Commitment to Germany, 1949–1955," in *American Historians and the Atlantic Alliance*, ed. Lawrence S. Kaplan (Kent, Ohio: Kent State University Press, 1991), 52–70.

[26]Schwarz, *Adenauer*, vol. 1, 589–99.

[27]Dinan, *Europe Recast*, 57–61; Rioux, *Fourth Republic*, 224–31.

[28]Duchêne, *Monnet*, 256–57.

[29]Ibid., 253–62; Hitchcock, *France Restored*, 203; Dinan, *Europe Recast*, 63–64.

[30]Duchêne, *Monnet*, 226–57; Ernst Haas, *The Uniting of Europe: Political, Social, and Economic Forces* (Stanford, Calif.: Stanford University Press, 1958).

[31]John Gillingham, "Solving the Ruhr Problem: German Heavy Industry and the Schuman Plan," in *The Beginnings of the Schuman Plan, 1950–51*, ed. Klaus Schwabe (Baden-Baden: Nomos Verlagsgeselschaft, 1988), 399–436.

[32]Schwarz, *Adenauer*, vol. 2, 118–32; Rioux, *Fourth Republic*, 231–33; Anthony Eden, *Full Circle: The Memoirs of Sir Anthony Eden* (London: Cassell, 1960), 165–71.

[33]May, "American Commitment," 52–80.

[34]Dinan, *Europe Recast*, 63–64; Urwin, *Community*, 58–74.

[35]Andrew Moravcsik, *The Choice for Europe: Social Purpose and State Power from Messina to Maastricht* (Ithaca, N.Y.: Cornell University Press, 1998), 86–87.

[36]Duchêne, *Monnet*, 262–69; Dinan, *Europe Recast*, 63–66.

[37]Duchêne, *Monnet*, 262–63; Dinan, *Europe Recast*, 66–67.

[38]Duchêne, *Monnet*, 292–306; Monnet, *Memoirs*, 412–19.

[39]Duchêne, *Monnet*, 274–83; Gilbert, *Surpassing Realism*, 62–65; Dinan, *Europe Recast*, 67–68.

[40]Duchêne, *Monnet*, 279–83; Gilbert, *Surpassing Realism*, 64–65; Dinan, *Europe Recast*, 66–69.

[41]Duchêne, *Monnet*, 285–88, 293–94; Maria Grazia Melchionni, "Le Comité d'Action pour les États-unis d'Europe: un réseau au service de l'union européenne," in *Jean Monnet: L'Europe et les chemins de la paix*, ed. Gérard Bossuat and Andreas Wilkens (Paris: Publications de la Sorbonne, 1999), 221–51.

[42]Spaak, *Continuing Battle*, 239. See Document 34.

[43]Gilbert, *Surpassing Realism*, 65–66; Dinan, *Europe Recast*, 66–70.

[44]Dinan, *Europe Recast*, 72–74.

[45]Ibid., 64–75.

[46]Texts of the treaties are available at http://eur-lex.europa.eu/en/treaties/index.htm and http://www.iue.it/; also in *Treaties Establishing the European Communities (ECSC, EEC, EAEC), Single European Act, Other Basic Instruments*, abr. ed. (Luxembourg: Office for Official Publications of the European Communities, 1987).

[47]Spaak, *Continuing Battle*, 251; Urwin, *Community*, 75–76.

[48]Dinan, *Europe Recast*, 76–77; Gilbert, *Surpassing Realism*, 69–75.

[49]Dinan, *Europe Recast*, 76–77.

[50]Hanns Jurgen Kusters, "The Treaties of Rome," in *The Dynamics of European Union*, ed. Roy Price (London: Croom Helm, 1987), 78–104; Urwin, *Community*, 77–84.

[51]Urwin, *Community*, 77–84; Dinan, *Europe Recast*, 76–77.

[52]Gilbert, *Surpassing Realism*, 10–11. See also Alan S. Milward, *The Reconstruction of Western Europe, 1945–51* (Berkeley: University of California Press, 1984), 462–502.

[53]Robert Marjolin, *Architect of European Unity: Memoirs, 1911–1986* (London: Weidenfeld and Nicolson, 1989), 306.

[54]Urwin, *Community*, 78–87; Dinan, *Europe Recast*, 83–90.

[55]Urwin, *Community*, 78–87.

[56]Stanley Hoffmann, "The Foreign Policy of Charles de Gaulle," in *The Diplomats, 1939–1979*, ed. Gordon Craig and Francis Loewenheim (Princeton, N.J.: Princeton University Press, 1994); Stanley Hoffmann, "The Man Who Would Be France," *New Republic*, December 17, 1990, 29–35.

[57]Dinan, *Europe Recast*, 90–93.

[58]Dinan, *Europe Recast*, 89–94; Alan S. Milward, *The European Rescue of the Nation-State* (Berkeley: University of California Press, 1992), 345–447. Miriam Camps, *Britain and the European Community, 1955–1963* (Princeton, N.J.: Princeton University Press, 1964).

[59]Jean Lacouture, *De Gaulle: The Ruler, 1945–1970* (New York: W. W. Norton, 1992), 350–62; Dinan, *Europe Recast*, 94–102; Moravcsik, *Choice*, 159–237.

[60]Douglas Brinkley, "Dean Acheson and John Kennedy: Combating Strains in the Atlantic Alliance, 1962–1963," in *John F. Kennedy and Europe*, ed. Douglas Brinkley and Richard Griffiths (Baton Rouge: Louisiana State University Press, 1999), 288–309; Pascaline Winand, *Eisenhower, Kennedy, and the United States of Europe* (New York: St. Martin's Press, 1993), 332–50.

[61]Schwarz, *Adenauer*, 2:596–687; author's interview with Hans-Peter Schwarz, September 23, 2003.

[62]Schwarz, *Adenauer*, 2:596–687; Dinan, *Europe Recast*, 102–3.

[63] *Foreign Relations of the United States (FRUS)*, 1961–1963, XIII, 146–48.

[64] Duchêne, *Monnet*, 315–33.

[65] Georges-Henri Soutou, *The French Military Program for Nuclear Energy, 1945–1981*. Occasional Paper 3, Nuclear History Program, University of Maryland, College Park, 1989.

[66] From the preamble to the Treaty of Rome, March 25, 1957, which states that the signatories are "determined to lay the foundations of an ever closer union among the peoples of Europe" (*Treaties Establishing the European Communities*).

[67] Dinan, *Europe Recast*, 10.

[68] Andrew Moravcsik, "A Too Perfect Union? Why Europe Said 'No,'" *Current History* (November 2005): 355.

[69] Gilbert, *Surpassing Realism*, 1, 4.

[70] Speech given by John Bruton, EU Ambassador to the United States, at the Woodrow Wilson International Center, March 3, 2005.

[71] After the Merger Treaty, signed by the EEC members on April 8, 1965, and entered into force on July 1, 1967, which fused the executives of the EEC, the ECSC, and Euratom and thereby created a single council and a single commission of the European Communities, the EEC became known as the European Community (EC).

[72] Milada Vachudova, *Europe Undivided* (New York: Oxford University Press, 2005), 1–24, 105–259.

[73] Dinan, *Europe Recast*, 1–11.

[74] Ibid., 83–229.

[75] Gilbert, *Surpassing Realism*, 119–51.

[76] Robert Kagan, *Of Paradise and Power: America and the New World Order* (New York: Vintage Books, 2004).

PART TWO

The Documents

1

War's Aftermath: Plans for Peace, Cold War, and Reconstruction

1

ALTIERO SPINELLI

The State of Federalism in June 1945

June 17, 1945

Altiero Spinelli, a popular Italian resistance leader and leading European federalist, called for a "free and united Europe" in the Ventotene Manifesto he drafted in June 1941 while exiled for antifascist activities. In 1943, he founded the European Federalist Movement in Milan and, along with other Italian activists, inspired the resistance representatives at a secret meeting in Geneva in the summer of 1944 to adopt the Draft Declaration of the European Resistance. The document stressed the need for a strong federal government of Europe. In the tradition of Italian federalism, the proposed union included Germany to ensure peace. In this 1945 article excerpted here for the newspaper run by his own circle of followers, Spinelli wrote about the direction European federalism should take in order to build a federalist perspective.

Having reached the end of the war, if we turn our attention to past events and consider once again what is the sole rational solution of the many problems of European civilization, we must again conclude that Europe can become an element of order in the world and a bastion of

Altiero Spinelli, "Bilancio federalista nel guigno 1945," *Italia Libera*, in *Documents on the History of European Integration*, ed. Walter Lipgens and Wilfried Loth (Berlin: Walter de Gruyter, 1988), 3:145–48.

law, liberty and well-being, only if there is an effective limitation of the sovereignty of its component states and if they are united in a federation. . . .

The state of European politics today is quite different from what it was at the end of the First World War. . . .

. . . The German army did not disintegrate after one or two big battles, leaving a political void in place of its short-lived barbaric empire: it retreated gradually till it held only a province, a town, or finally an underground bunker. The liberated countries have not been allowed to manage their own affairs, but have been systematically occupied, controlled and put under tutelage by the three great powers. These powers have supported this or that political tendency in the countries they respectively occupied, but in every case they have restored the states to what they were before the Nazi aggression. The great powers too have for the time being deprived them *de facto* or *de jure* of any possibility of developing their own foreign policy. The consequence of this tutelage by the USSR, the USA and Britain is that the European countries have at present no opportunity of exercising any initiative. . . .

. . . Therefore the integration of the European nations into one free community can take place only when the great powers have reached a settlement which allows the European nations, or at least a considerable number of them, to regain some freedom of action, so that they can give thought to joint efforts to achieve their common destiny.

Given this world situation, the need for collaboration among European peoples to re-establish a civilized order on the continent is such that there will in future be many opportunities, as there have been in the past, to do away with traditional national patterns and work out a higher political organization. The real, profound obstacle to the development of federalism in Europe is not the present more or less temporary phase of tutelage but the difficulty for the European nations, and especially their governing classes, to consider national problems in terms of their common European civilization, and their automatic tendency to consider problems of international coexistence merely in terms of national power. It cannot even be said that if the tutelage of the three great powers were removed, the European states would find it easier to come to terms with one another. . . .

The earthquake that has convulsed the material and political life of the continent has not been matched by a similar earthquake of the spirit. It is true that deep fissures already exist in the minds of all politicians of the different countries and of the masses who follow them. But these fissures are not yet visible, and people themselves are hardly aware of them. Time will be needed to bring them to the surface. Today everyone is anxious to improve this or that aspect of national life, but people fail to recognize that national problems can only be solved on a supranational basis. . . .

. . . We shall follow attentively the development of relations between Russia, America and Britain, pointing out to public opinion the favorable and unfavorable occasions that may present themselves from time to time for the creation of an international federal system. But above all, in collaboration with all those in Italy and abroad who realize that the age of nationalism must be buried once and for all, we shall endeavor to break the rigid mold of nationalist tradition and form a political consciousness capable of understanding events and building on them in a federalist perspective. Until such a political consciousness takes shape, any opportunities that occur will vanish to no purpose, like those that have presented themselves in the past.

2

RAYMOND ARON

"If France Does Not Recover . . . What Hope Is There for Europe?"

July 1945

Raymond Aron was an influential French political philosopher, sociologist, journalist, and commentator. He believed that transatlantic cooperation was important in the search for a just international order. In this excerpt from his book, Aron argued that France must reform internally in order to restore its international position and "a sense of unity" to Europe without sacrificing its rich heritage of diversity. Cooperation between France and Britain was essential to achieve his goal of a unified Europe working with the United States. In 1948, he advocated a union of Western Europe, including West Germany, to resist Soviet domination.

Raymond Aron, *L'âge des empires et l'avenir de la France* (Paris, 1945), 23–27, 253ff, in *Documents on the History of European Integration*, ed. Walter Lipgens and Wilfried Loth (Berlin: Walter de Gruyter, 1988), 3:31–34.

The French crisis tends to merge into the crisis of our continent as a whole. For various reasons France's expansion in the nineteenth century, on the human and individual level, lagged behind that of other great countries. But now that Germany has been overthrown and mutilated, and Britain brought closer to the continent by the development of aviation, the V1's and V2's[1] and other inventions yet to come, we can see that France's backwardness is only an extreme form of the backwardness of all nation states. The arrival on the scene of multinational, continental states has in a sense aggravated the backwardness of our country, but it has also given us a better chance of recovery provided we link our fate to that of others.

If we despair of France, therefore, we must also despair of Europe. If France does not recover, what other country would play the part that history offers us? If France is done for, what hope is there for Europe, drenched in blood and covered by ruins? . . .

There is an essential ambiguity in the situation. The governing principle is to enlarge economic and political units without abolishing the nation state or superseding the patriotism by which our historical groups are knit together. But it is utopian to envisage a union of the whole of Western Europe, including Germany and Italy as well as France, Spain and Britain. One can imagine a system combining respect for nationalities with the economic and military advantages of empire; but for the time being such an idea is no less vague than attractive. . . .

Our first and most urgent task is internal reform. A country influences the world by what it is, not by the flattering picture that propagandists seek to present to outsiders. Unless France puts her house in order there will be no hope for her, either in alliances or in a Western bloc, because she will have lost the ability to exist by herself as a political community. If, on the other hand, she recovers her strength and will-power, her efforts and sacrifices will be fitly rewarded. She will be able to take part, and a major part, in the work which Germany tried to accomplish by inhuman means and which the defeat of the Third Reich has bequeathed to us: that of restoring to Europe a sense of unity without sacrificing its heritage of rich and fruitful diversity.

France, the first model of the nation state, is now sharing in the decline of Europe and of nationalities. Is it not her mission to save the nation states and to save Europe, by helping the states to transcend themselves and by helping Europe to recover a sense of unity?

To the west of those lands that are governed by Soviet force and prestige there is a population of between 200 and 250 million of the

[1]German surface-to-surface rockets known as "buzz bombs."

most civilized inhabitants of the globe, with huge industrial possibilities. They belong, as we know, to different states, some of which are divided by traditional prejudice or deep-seated hostility. No miracle is going to substitute order for chaos all at once; but to transcend national states without obliterating them is a historic task to which France can and should make a unique contribution.

How, and to what extent, this task can be accomplished is a matter for another study, to which the present essay may be regarded as a mere introduction. Let us only conclude by saying that constant and trusting cooperation between Britain and France will be an indispensable condition. The less we speak of a Western bloc, the better; it is an idea that arouses too much passion and opposition. But if our two countries can find a means, in practical day-to-day terms, of speaking with one voice and acting in unison, then there will be a hope of resurrection for our war-torn continent.

3

JEAN MONNET

"The French Economy Can't Be Transformed Unless the French People Take Part . . . in an Investment and Modernization Plan"

August 1945

International investment banker and French emissary to the United States Jean Monnet was head of the French Supply Council from 1943 to 1945. The council's job was to purchase provisions through U.S. government programs for the Allied forces in France by selecting products, organizing their transport, and negotiating their payment. Monnet believed that France required drastic measures to reconstruct and renovate its enfeebled economy after the war. In these excerpts Monnet described a conversation with provisional French president Charles de Gaulle in Washington in August 1945, in which Monnet claimed that he convinced de Gaulle of the need to rebuild France in a systematic way.

Jean Monnet, *Memoirs* (Garden City, N.Y.: Doubleday, 1978), 232–35.

The French government adopted the Monnet Plan for reconstruction in January 1947.

It was obvious to everyone that France had emerged from the war severely weakened. Less well known, or less willingly acknowledged, was the weakness from which she was already suffering when war broke out. This, no less than military or moral shortcomings, explained her sudden collapse in 1940. A few weeks after my return to France, [Robert] Marjolin, [Etienne] Hirsch, and I looked at the figures. No one had previously put them together and faced the grim picture they revealed: the slow and regular decline of our economy. Fierce controversies about the neglect of spiritual values in recent years, and the ardent professions of faith in the future made by the country's new leaders—none of these touched the fundamentals of France's problem. Its origins lay far back in time, and its solution would not be found overnight. The Liberation had given us back our freedom, but with all its liabilities and with heavy debts. When I had promised General de Gaulle in Washington that I would tackle the modernization of France, I had had no idea how huge a task it would be. Now, I realized that it was vital: it would occupy all my energies and those of the men who had worked with me on the war effort. To sustain a comparable effort in peacetime, we should once again need to take an overall view and to mobilize all available human and material resources. The arsenal of victory and the powerhouse of reconstruction had this in common: each in its turn was engaged in the same fight against fatalism. . . .

. . . The low level of production and national wealth was itself only a symptom of our enfeeblement, which the two world wars had merely made worse. The deeper reason was undoubtedly the lack of enterprise, which had led to a serious neglect of productive investment and modernization. This in turn had affected the level of economic activity, which was now barely enough to meet the needs of domestic consumption. . . .

I realized that we should have to disappoint those who believed that the Liberation would bring prosperity. For four years, they had lived on idealized memories or impatient hopes; but the basis of the prosperity they dreamed of had been forgotten for too long to be restored so quickly. A long campaign of explanation would be needed before the country could be persuaded to invest in essential capital goods rather than squander its resources on immediate satisfactions. But we had to do more than just return to prewar standards, which had been modest; and there was a danger that the country would slacken before it fully caught up. This psychological problem seemed to me all-important, and I spoke about it to General de Gaulle. He too, I found, was anxious to ensure that we should not relax our efforts.

"It will take time," I said, "to rebuild our cities and ports and to repair the railways. But all this will be done, because there is no alternative. On the other hand, it will take very great willpower and an immense effort of explanation before people realize what is really wrong—which is that our capital equipment and production methods are out of date."

"That is a task for the authorities," he answered. "Make a proposal to them."

"I don't know exactly what has to be done," I said; "but I'm sure of one thing. The French economy can't be transformed unless the French people take part in its transformation. And when I say 'the French people,' I don't mean an abstract entity: I mean trade unionists, industrialists, and civil servants. Everyone must be associated in an investment and modernization plan."

"That is what has to be done, and that is the name for it," de Gaulle concluded. "Send me your proposals before the end of the year."

4

WINSTON CHURCHILL

Iron Curtain Speech

March 5, 1946

Winston Churchill, Britain's wartime prime minister, delivered what has become one of his most famous speeches at Westminster College in Fulton, Missouri, where he was awarded an honorary degree. After Churchill's Conservative party was defeated in 1945, he became leader of the Opposition. Introduced by President Harry Truman at Westminster,

Winston S. Churchill: His Complete Speeches, 1897–1963, ed. Robert Rhodes James (London: Chelsea House, 1974), 7:7285–93.

Churchill called for a special relationship between the United States and the British Commonwealth to defeat the great dangers he said faced the free world: tyranny and war. To prevent another war, Churchill argued, a strong United Nations organization must work to reach a "good understanding" with the Soviet Union, which had divided Europe. Part of Churchill's speech is reprinted here.

A shadow has fallen upon the scenes so lately lighted by the Allied victory. Nobody knows what Soviet Russia and its Communist international organization intends to do in the immediate future, or what are the limits, if any, to their expansive and proselytizing tendencies. I have a strong admiration and regard for the valiant Russian people and for my wartime comrade, Marshal Stalin. There is deep sympathy and goodwill in Britain—and I doubt not here also—towards the peoples of all the Russias and a resolve to persevere through many differences and rebuffs in establishing lasting friendships. We understand the Russian need to be secure on her western frontiers by the removal of all possibility of German aggression. We welcome Russia to her rightful place among the leading nations of the world. We welcome her flag upon the seas. Above all, we welcome constant, frequent and growing contacts between the Russian people and our own people on both sides of the Atlantic. It is my duty however, for I am sure you would wish me to state the facts as I see them to you, to place before you certain facts about the present position in Europe.

From Stettin in the Baltic to Trieste in the Adriatic, an iron curtain has descended across the Continent. Behind that line lie all the capitals of the ancient states of Central and Eastern Europe. Warsaw, Berlin, Prague, Vienna, Budapest, Belgrade, Bucharest and Sofia, all these famous cities and the populations around them lie in what I must call the Soviet sphere, and all are subject in one form or another, not only to Soviet influence but to a very high and, in many cases, increasing measure of control from Moscow. Athens alone—Greece with its immortal glories—is free to decide its future at an election under British, American and French observation. The Russian-dominated Polish Government has been encouraged to make enormous and wrongful inroads upon Germany, and mass expulsions of millions of Germans on a scale grievous and undreamed-of are now taking place. The Communist parties, which were very small in all these Eastern States of Europe, have been raised to pre-eminence and power far beyond their numbers and are seeking everywhere to obtain totalitarian control. Police governments are prevailing in nearly every case, and so far, except in Czechoslovakia, there is no true democracy. . . .

The safety of the world requires a new unity in Europe, from which no nation should be permanently outcast. It is from the quarrels of the strong parent races in Europe that the world wars we have witnessed, or which occurred in former times, have sprung. Twice in our own lifetime we have seen the United States, against their wishes and their traditions, against arguments, the force of which it is impossible not to comprehend, drawn by irresistible forces, into these wars in time to secure the victory of the good cause, but only after frightful slaughter and devastation had occurred. Twice the United States has had to send several millions of its young men across the Atlantic to find the war; but now war can find any nation, wherever it may dwell between dusk and dawn. Surely we should work with conscious purpose for a grand pacification of Europe, within the structure of the United Nations and in accordance with its Charter. That I feel is an open cause of policy of very great importance. . . .

. . . I repulse the idea that a new war is inevitable; still more that it is imminent. It is because I am sure that our fortunes are still in our own hands and that we hold the power to save the future, that I feel the duty to speak out now that I have the occasion and the opportunity to do so. I do not believe that Soviet Russia desires war. What they desire is the fruits of war and the indefinite expansion of their power and doctrines. But what we have to consider here to-day while time remains, is the permanent prevention of war and the establishment of conditions of freedom and democracy as rapidly as possible in all countries. Our difficulties and dangers will not be removed by closing our eyes to them. They will not be removed by mere waiting to see what happens; nor will they be removed by a policy of appeasement. What is needed is a settlement, and the longer this is delayed, the more difficult it will be and the greater our dangers will become.

. . . If the Western Democracies stand together in strict adherence to the principles of the United Nations Charter, their influence for furthering those principles will be immense and no one is likely to molest them. If however they become divided or falter in their duty and if these all-important years are allowed to slip away then indeed catastrophe may overwhelm us all.

Last time I saw it all coming and cried aloud to my own fellow-countrymen and to the world, but no one paid any attention. . . . We surely must not let that happen again. This can only be achieved by reaching now, in 1946, a good understanding on all points with Russia under the general authority of the United Nations Organization and by the maintenance of that good understanding through many peaceful years, by the world instrument, supported by the whole strength of the English-speaking world and all its connections. There is the solution which I respectfully offer to you in this Address to which I have given the title "The Sinews of Peace."

... If the population of the English-speaking Commonwealths be added to that of the United States with all that such co-operation implies in the air, on the sea, all over the globe and in science and in industry, and in moral force, there will be no quivering, precarious balance of power to offer its temptation to ambition or adventure. On the contrary, there will be an overwhelming assurance of security. If we adhere faithfully to the Charter of the United Nations and walk forward in sedate and sober strength seeking no one's land or treasure, seeking to lay no arbitrary control upon the thoughts of men; if all British moral and material forces and convictions are joined with your own in fraternal association, the high-roads of the future will be clear, not only for us but for all, not only for our time, but for a century to come.

5

WINSTON CHURCHILL

United States of Europe Speech

September 19, 1946

Churchill's call for a United States of Europe and a partnership between France and Germany had a great influence on political leaders and postwar integration activists. Although he did not offer a detailed plan for achieving unity, Churchill's speech at Zurich University motivated others to organize the Congress of Europe in May 1948 and the Council of Europe in May 1949, both important steps in European integration.

Winston S. Churchill: His Complete Speeches, 1897–1963, ed. Robert Rhodes James (London: Chelsea House, 1974), 7:7379–82.

I wish to speak to you to-day about the tragedy of Europe. This noble continent, comprising on the whole the fairest and the most cultivated regions of the earth, enjoying a temperate and equable climate, is the home of all the great parent races of the western world. It is the fountain of Christian faith and Christian ethics. It is the origin of most of the culture, arts, philosophy and science both of ancient and modern times. If Europe were once united in the sharing of its common inheritance, there would be no limit to the happiness, to the prosperity and glory which its three or four hundred million people would enjoy. Yet it is from Europe that have sprung that series of frightful nationalistic quarrels, originated by the Teutonic nations, which we have seen even in this twentieth century and in our own lifetime, wreck the peace and mar the prospects of all mankind.

And what is the plight to which Europe has been reduced? Some of the smaller States have indeed made a good recovery, but over wide areas a vast quivering mass of tormented, hungry, care-worn and bewildered human beings gape at the ruins of their cities and homes, and scan the dark horizons for the approach of some new peril, tyranny or terror. Among the victors there is a babel of jarring voices; among the vanquished the sullen silence of despair. That is all that Europeans, grouped in so many ancient States and nations, that is all that the Germanic Powers have got by tearing each other to pieces and spreading havoc far and wide. Indeed, but for the fact that the great Republic across the Atlantic Ocean has at length realized that the ruin or enslavement of Europe would involve their own fate as well, and has stretched out hands of succor and guidance, the Dark Ages would have returned in all their cruelty and squalor. They may still return.

Yet all the while there is a remedy which, if it were generally and spontaneously adopted, would as if by a miracle transform the whole scene, and would in a few years make all Europe, or the greater part of it, as free and as happy as Switzerland is to-day. What is this sovereign remedy? It is to re-create the European Family, or as much of it as we can, and provide it with a structure under which it can dwell in peace, in safety and in freedom. We must build a kind of United States of Europe. In this way only will hundreds of millions of toilers be able to regain the simple joys and hopes which make life worth living. The process is simple. All that is needed is the resolve of hundreds of millions of men and women to do right instead of wrong and gain as their reward blessing instead of cursing.

Much work has been done upon this task by the exertions of the

Pan-European Union which owes so much to Count Coudenhove-Kalergi[1] and which commanded the services of the famous French patriot and statesman, Aristide Briand. There is also that immense body of doctrine and procedure, which was brought into being amid high hopes after the first world war, as the League of Nations. The League of Nations did not fail because of its principles or conceptions. It failed because these principles were deserted by those States who had brought it into being. It failed because the Governments of those days feared to face the facts, and act while time remained. This disaster must not be repeated. There is therefore much knowledge and material with which to build; and also bitter dear-bought experience.

I was very glad to read in the newspapers two days ago that my friend President Truman had expressed his interest and sympathy with this great design. There is no reason why a regional organization of Europe should in any way conflict with the world organization of the United Nations. On the contrary, I believe that the larger synthesis will only survive if it is founded upon coherent natural groupings. There is already a natural grouping in the Western Hemisphere. We British have our own Commonwealth of Nations. These do not weaken, on the contrary they strengthen, the world organization. They are in fact its main support. And why should there not be a European group which could give a sense of enlarged patriotism and common citizenship to the distracted peoples of this turbulent and mighty continent and why should it not take its rightful place with other great groupings in shaping the destinies of men? In order that this should be accomplished there must be an act of faith in which millions of families speaking many languages must consciously take part.

We all know that the two world wars through which we have passed arose out of the vain passion of a newly-united Germany to play the dominating part in the world. In this last struggle crimes and massacres have been committed for which there is no parallel since the invasions of the Mongols in the fourteenth century and no equal at any time in human history. The guilty must be punished. Germany must be deprived of the power to rearm and make another aggressive war. But when all this has been done, as it will be done, as it is being done, there must be an end to retribution. There must be what Mr. Gladstone[2] many years ago called "a blessed act of oblivion." We must

[1]Austrian aristocrat and founder of the Pan-European Union in 1923 who argued for a European federation to further integration and international cooperation.

all turn our backs upon the horrors of the past. We must look to the future. We cannot afford to drag forward across the years that are to come the hatreds and revenges which have sprung from the injuries of the past. If Europe is to be saved from infinite misery, and indeed from final doom, there must be an act of faith in the European family and an act of oblivion against all the crimes and follies of the past.

Can the free peoples of Europe rise to the height of these resolves of the soul and instincts of the spirit of man? If they can, the wrongs and injuries which have been inflicted will have been washed away on all sides by the miseries which have been endured. Is there any need for further floods of agony? Is it the only lesson of history that mankind is unteachable? Let there be justice, mercy and freedom. The peoples have only to will it, and all will achieve their hearts' desire.

I am now going to say something that will astonish you. The first step in the re-creation of the European family must be a partnership between France and Germany. In this way only can France recover the moral leadership of Europe. There can be no revival of Europe without a spiritually great France and a spiritually great Germany. The structure of the United States of Europe, if well and truly built, will be such as to make the material strength of a single state less important. Small nations will count as much as large ones and gain their honor by their contribution to the common cause. The ancient states and principalities of Germany, freely joined together for mutual convenience in a federal system, might each take their individual place among the United States of Europe. I shall not try to make a detailed program for hundreds of millions of people who want to be happy and free, prosperous and safe, who wish to enjoy the four freedoms of which the great President Roosevelt spoke, and live in accordance with the principles embodied in the Atlantic Charter. If this is their wish, they have only to say so, and means can certainly be found, and machinery erected, to carry that wish into full fruition.

But I must give you a warning. Time may be short. At present there is a breathing-space. The cannon have ceased firing. The fighting has stopped; but the dangers have not stopped. If we are to form the United States of Europe or whatever name or form it may take, we must begin now.

In these present days we dwell strangely and precariously under the shield and protection of the atomic bomb. The atomic bomb is still

[2]William E. Gladstone, British prime minister, 1868–1874, 1880–1885, 1886, and 1892–1894.

only in the hands of a State and nation which we know will never use it except in the cause of right and freedom. But it may well be that in a few years this awful agency of destruction will be widespread and the catastrophe following from its use by several warring nations will not only bring to an end all that we call civilization, but may possibly disintegrate the globe itself.

I must now sum up the propositions which are before you. Our constant aim must be to build and fortify the strength of U.N.O. [United Nations Organization]. Under and within that world concept we must re-create the European family in a regional structure called, it may be, the United States of Europe. The first step is to form a Council of Europe. If at first all the States of Europe are not willing or able to join the Union, we must nevertheless proceed to assemble and combine those who will and those who can. The salvation of the common people of every race and of every land from war or servitude must be established on solid foundations and must be guarded by the readiness of all men and women to die rather than submit to tyranny. In all this urgent work, France and Germany must take the lead together. Great Britain, the British Commonwealth of Nations, mighty America, and I trust Soviet Russia—for then indeed all would be well—must be the friends and sponsors of the new Europe and must champion its right to live and shine.

6

HARRY TRUMAN

The Truman Doctrine

March 12, 1947

Taking up burdens Britain could no longer carry, President Harry Truman went before a joint session of Congress in March 1947 to ask for economic and military aid for Greece ($250 million) and Turkey ($150 million) and announced the Truman Doctrine. It implied an American

Harry Truman, *Public Papers of the Presidents of the United States: Harry Truman, 1947* (Washington, D.C.: Government Printing Office, 1963), 176–80.

commitment to assist other nations threatened by Communist intimidation, internal subversion, or external aggression throughout the world. Congress approved the bill, and Truman signed it into law in late May. The policy of containment of the Soviet Union outlined in this excerpt provided a rationale for continued American activism in Europe and paved the way for the Marshall Plan.

The gravity of the situation which confronts the world today necessitates my appearance before a joint session of the Congress.

The foreign policy and the national security of this country are involved.

One aspect of the present situation, which I present to you at this time for your consideration and decision, concerns Greece and Turkey.

The United States has received from the Greek Government an urgent appeal for financial and economic assistance. Preliminary reports from the American Economic Mission now in Greece and reports from the American Ambassador in Greece corroborate the statement of the Greek Government that assistance is imperative if Greece is to survive as a free nation. . . .

The very existence of the Greek state is today threatened by the terrorist activities of several thousand armed men, led by Communists, who defy the government's authority at a number of points, particularly along the northern boundaries. A Commission appointed by the United Nations Security Council is at present investigating disturbed conditions in northern Greece and alleged border violations along the frontier between Greece on the one hand and Albania, Bulgaria, and Yugoslavia on the other.

Meanwhile, the Greek Government is unable to cope with the situation. The Greek army is small and poorly equipped. It needs supplies and equipment if it is to restore authority to the government throughout Greek territory.

Greece must have assistance if it is to become a self-supporting and self-respecting democracy.

The United States must supply this assistance. We have already extended to Greece certain types of relief and economic aid but these are inadequate.

There is no other country to which democratic Greece can turn. . . .

The Greek Government has been operating in an atmosphere of chaos and extremism. It has made mistakes. The extension of aid by this country does not mean that the United States condones everything that the Greek Government has done or will do. We have condemned in the past, and we condemn now, extremist measures of the right or the left. We have in the past advised tolerance, and we advise tolerance now. . . .

The future of Turkey as an independent and economically sound state is clearly no less important to the freedom-loving peoples of the world than the future of Greece. The circumstances in which Turkey finds itself today are considerably different from those of Greece. Turkey has been spared the disasters that have beset Greece. And during the war, the United States and Great Britain furnished Turkey with material aid.

Nevertheless, Turkey now needs our support.

Since the war Turkey has sought additional financial assistance from Great Britain and the United States for the purpose of effecting that modernization necessary for the maintenance of its national integrity.

That integrity is essential to the preservation of order in the Middle East.

The British Government has informed us that, owing to its own difficulties, it can no longer extend financial or economic aid to Turkey.

As in the case of Greece, if Turkey is to have the assistance it needs, the United States must supply it. We are the only country able to provide that help. . . .

I believe that it must be the policy of the United States to support free peoples who are resisting attempted subjugation by armed minorities or by outside pressures.

I believe that we must assist free peoples to work out their own destinies in their own way.

I believe that our help should be primarily through economic and financial aid which is essential to economic stability and orderly political processes. . . .

The seeds of totalitarian regimes are nurtured by misery and want. They spread and grow in the evil soil of poverty and strife. They reach their full growth when the hope of a people for a better life has died.

We must keep that hope alive.

The free peoples of the world look to us for support in maintaining their freedoms.

If we falter in our leadership, we may endanger the peace of the world—and we shall surely endanger the welfare of this Nation.

Great responsibilities have been placed upon us by the swift movement of events.

I am confident that the Congress will face these responsibilities squarely.

7

GEORGE C. MARSHALL

"The World Situation Is Very Serious"

June 5, 1947

At Harvard University's 1947 commencement, U.S. secretary of state George Marshall presented a picture of Europe's economy in a state of disintegration and declared that the United States was committed to the reconstruction of Europe. This announcement signaled the Truman administration's strategy to create an alternative to communism and diminish its appeal by improving the desperate economic and social conditions. Marshall insisted that Europeans take the initiative to cooperate and design their own regional recovery program. The following March, Congress passed the Economic Cooperation Act of 1948, which embodied the Marshall Plan, or the European Recovery Program, as it was formally named.

I need not tell you gentlemen that the world situation is very serious. That must be apparent to all intelligent people. I think one difficulty is that the problem is one of such enormous complexity that the very mass of facts presented to the public by press and radio make it exceedingly difficult for the man in the street to reach a clear appraisement of the situation. Furthermore, the people of this country are distant from the troubled areas of the earth and it is hard for them to comprehend the plight and consequent reactions of the long-suffering

Foreign Relations of the United States, 1947, III, 237–39.

peoples, and the effect of those reactions on their governments in connection with our efforts to promote peace in the world.

In considering the requirements for the rehabilitation of Europe the physical loss of life, the visible destruction of cities, factories, mines and railroads was correctly estimated, but it has become obvious during recent months that this visible destruction was probably less serious than the dislocation of the entire fabric of European economy. For the past ten years conditions have been highly abnormal. The feverish preparation for war and the more feverish maintenance of the war effort engulfed all aspects of national economies. Machinery has fallen into disrepair or is entirely obsolete. Under the arbitrary and destructive Nazi rule, virtually every possible enterprise was geared into the German war machine. Long-standing commercial ties, private institutions, banks, insurance companies and shipping companies disappeared, through loss of capital, absorption through nationalization or by simple destruction. In many countries, confidence in the local currency has been severely shaken. The breakdown of the business structure of Europe during the war was complete. Recovery has been seriously retarded by the fact that two years after the close of hostilities a peace settlement with Germany and Austria has not be agreed upon. But even given a more prompt solution of these difficult problems, the rehabilitation of the economic structure of Europe quite evidently will require a much longer time and greater effort than had been foreseen.

There is a phase of this matter which is both interesting and serious. The farmer has always produced the foodstuffs to exchange with the city dweller for the other necessities of life. This division of labor is the basis of modern civilization. At the present time it is threatened with breakdown. The town and city industries are not producing adequate goods to exchange with the food-producing farmer. Raw materials and fuel are in short supply. Machinery is lacking or worn out. The farmer or the peasant cannot find the goods for sale which he desires to purchase. So the sale of his farm produce for money which he cannot use seems to him an unprofitable transaction. He, therefore, has withdrawn many fields from crop cultivation and is using them for grazing. He feeds more grain to stock and finds for himself and his family an ample supply of food, however short he may be on clothing and the other ordinary gadgets of civilization. Meanwhile people in the cities are short of food and fuel. So the governments are forced to use their foreign money and credits to procure these necessities abroad. This process exhausts funds which are urgently needed for reconstruction. Thus a very serious situation is rapidly developing which bodes no good for the world. The modern system of the division of labor upon which the exchange of products is based is in danger of breaking down.

The truth of the matter is that Europe's requirements for the next three or four years of foreign food and other essential products—principally from America—are so much greater than her present ability to pay that she must have substantial additional help, or face economic, social and political deterioration of a very grave character.

The remedy lies in breaking the vicious circle and restoring the confidence of the European people in the economic future of their own countries and of Europe as a whole. The manufacturer and the farmer throughout wide areas must be able and willing to exchange their products for currencies the continuing value of which is not open to question.

Aside from the demoralizing effect on the world at large and the possibilities of disturbances arising as a result of the desperation of the people concerned, the consequences to the economy of the United States should be apparent to all. It is logical that the United States should do whatever it is able to do to assist in the return of normal economic health in the world, without which there can be no political stability and no assured peace. Our policy is directed not against any country or doctrine but against hunger, poverty, desperation and chaos. Its purpose should be the revival of a working economy in the world so as to permit the emergence of political and social conditions in which free institutions can exist. Such assistance, I am convinced, must not be on a piece-meal basis as various crises develop. Any assistance that this Government may render in the future should provide a cure rather than a mere palliative. Any government that is willing to assist in the task of recovery will find full cooperation, I am sure, on the part of the United States Government. Any government which maneuvers to block the recovery of other countries cannot expect help from us. Furthermore, governments, political parties or groups which seek to perpetuate human misery in order to profit therefrom politically or otherwise will encounter the opposition of the United States.

It is already evident that, before the United States Government can proceed much further in its efforts to alleviate the situation and help start the European world on its way to recovery, there must be some agreement among the countries of Europe as to the requirements of the situation and the part those countries themselves will take in order to give proper effect to whatever action might be undertaken by this Government. It would be neither fitting nor efficacious for this Government to undertake to draw up unilaterally a program designed to place Europe on its feet economically. This is the business of the Europeans. The initiative, I think, must come from Europe. The role of this country should consist of friendly aid in the drafting of a European program and of later support of such a program so far as it may be practical for us to do so. The program should be a joint one, agreed to by a number, if not all European nations.

An essential part of any successful action on the part of the United States is an understanding on the part of the people of America of the character of the problem and the remedies to be applied. Political passion and prejudice should have no part. With foresight, and a willingness on the part of our people to face up to the vast responsibility which history has clearly placed upon our country, the difficulties I have outlined can and will be overcome.

8

ANDREI VYSHINSKY

Criticism of the Truman Doctrine and Marshall Plan

September 18, 1947

In a speech to the United Nations General Assembly, excerpted here, Andrei Vyshinsky, deputy to Soviet foreign minister Vyacheslav Molotov, declared that the Marshall Plan violated the principles of the United Nations and would result in American political and economic control over the recipient countries. At the invitation of the U.S. government, the Soviet Union had participated in initial discussions about receiving

UN General Assembly, Official Records, Plenary Meetings, September 18, 1947, 86–88.

Marshall Plan aid. But on July 2, 1947, Moscow announced that it would not attend the scheduled July 12 meeting in Paris for the sixteen recipient nations to begin planning for the comprehensive economic recovery program.

The so-called Truman Doctrine and the Marshall Plan are particularly glaring examples of the way in which the principles of the United Nations are violated, of the way in which the Organization is ignored. . . .

As is now clear, the Marshall Plan constitutes in essence merely a variant of the Truman Doctrine adapted to the conditions of postwar Europe. In bringing forward this plan, the United States Government apparently counted on the cooperation of the Governments of the United Kingdom and France to confront the European countries in need of relief with the necessity of renouncing their inalienable right to dispose of their economic resources and to plan their national economy in their own way. The United States also counted on making all these countries directly dependent on the interests of American monopolies, which are striving to avert the approaching depression by an accelerated export of commodities and capital to Europe. . . .

It is becoming more and more evident to everyone that the implementation of the Marshall Plan will mean placing European countries under the economic and political control of the United States and direct interference by the latter in the internal affairs of those countries.

Moreover, this plan is an attempt to split Europe into two camps and, with the help of the United Kingdom and France, to complete the formation of a *bloc* of several European countries hostile to the interests of the democratic countries of Eastern Europe and most particularly to the interests of the Soviet Union.

An important feature of this Plan is the attempt to confront the countries of Eastern Europe with a *bloc* of Western European States including Western Germany. The intention is to make use of Western Germany and German heavy industry (the Ruhr) as one of the most important economic bases for American expansion in Europe, in disregard of the national interests of the countries which suffered from German aggression.

9

ROBERT MARJOLIN

The Design and Goals of the Monnet Plan

1946–1948

Robert Marjolin played a key role in the design of the Monnet Plan. A brilliant young economist and socialist planner in the 1930s, this Frenchman became a close colleague of Monnet's during the war, first in London and later in Washington. From 1943 to 1945, he served as the staff economist of the French Supply Council and then succeeded Monnet as head of the council. In this excerpt from his memoirs, Marjolin, who became deputy planning commissioner, discussed the Monnet Plan's priorities and the methods used to implement it. The plan set France on the road to economic recovery, propagated the idea that modernization was essential for France, and enhanced Monnet's stature in Europe as well as in France.

It was no longer a question of catching up with the other developed countries, it had become necessary to reconstruct a country partly destroyed by the war, to modernize its plant made obsolete by the depression crisis and enemy occupation, to invest on an unprecedented scale when the nation would be clamoring for rapid satisfaction of consumer wants. In short, a plan was needed that would give priority to investment in general, and more particularly to capital expenditure that would lead the economy's development and make it possible to attain, after an initial phase of relative austerity, a level of consumption the French had never known. . . .

. . . For the country to emerge from the abyss into which it had been plunged by a history of backwardness in the movement towards industrialization, by a profound decline during the thirties, and then by the war and the Occupation, a number of conditions had to be fulfilled, some material, some psychological.

It was necessary, first of all, for the country, or at least its front-rank

---

Robert Marjolin, *Architect of European Unity: Memoirs, 1911–1986* (London: Weidenfeld and Nicolson, 1989), 161–70.

politicians, senior civil servants, trade union leaders and the representatives of industry and agriculture, to gain awareness of the effort to be accomplished. Reconstruction, to begin with, for it must not be forgotten that the damage sustained by France in World War Two was more than double what she suffered in World War One; but most important, a renewal of the nation's capital stock, which had been destroyed, depleted or reduced to obsolescence: France had to develop rapidly her heavy and engineering industries, not only to meet the population's needs and underpin exports but also to be able, if need be, to mass-produce modern armaments and thus play her part as a great power in the system of collective security. . . .

To put the investment effort into perspective, I added that for the period considered as a whole (1946–50), the share of national resources allocated to investment would amount to about 23–24%, against 19% in 1946, 16% in 1938 and 20% in 1929.

The division of labor in the team that Jean Monnet had gathered around him was effected without any difficulty. Monnet, whose deputy I was, relied on me for the overall design and general balance of the system we were trying to set up. Etienne Hirsch was responsible for the individual sectors of industry; it was his job to draw up a balance sheet of needs and resources for each of the major products on which the Plan's realization depended: coal, steel, cement, etc. Paul Delouvrier, who in the course of a brilliant career was notably to become chairman of the board of Electricité de France in 1969, was in charge of financial affairs. Jean Fourastié was the Plan's economic adviser. Alfred Sauvy, Félix Gaillard, Jacques Dumontier, and others, gave us valuable assistance.[1]

Of course, Monnet did not accept my conclusions without our having discussed them at length and, in some cases, my having been talked into amending them. As is the way with all strong minds, he appreciated resistance, even if it sometimes irritated him. I remember, though I cannot place it exactly in time, a discussion that lasted a whole afternoon and was, I think, about the Plan's targets. The discussion had become what I am tempted to call a passage of arms between Monnet and myself, the other participants in the meeting having reached the end of their arguments. Late in the evening, when we were all exhausted, Monnet wound up the discussion with these words: "Marjolin, the trouble with you is that you're an intellectual. All

[1] Paul Delouvrier and Félix Gaillard were senior civil servants. Jean Fourastié, Alfred Sauvy, and Jacques Dumontier were statisticians and economists.

right, I give in, but I want you to know that if I do it is not because you have been so insistent, but because I convinced myself, in spite of your cussedness, that you were right."

I mention this little incident because it illustrates the kind of relationship that had developed between Jean Monnet and me, the fighting spirit we showed, he and I, in our search for the truth, the great objectivity he was capable of demonstrating. Needless to say, the situation was frequently reversed; I, too, knew how to give in when his practical sense, which was nothing short of genius, enabled him to identify clearly the goal to be attained. . . .

. . . It was also necessary to establish an order of priorities in the allocation of savings, to give preference to a limited number of industries that would act as pacesetters for the economy, even if other activities had to be sacrificed temporarily. Housing, in the event, was one of the latter.

As it turned out, this order of priorities was inescapable. However one might visualize France's future growth, it presupposed a much bigger output of coal, steel, electricity, cement; transport facilities would have to be reconstructed and modernized; greatly increased quantities of food products, which would rapidly be needed, could be provided only by mechanized farming, which would necessitate a stock of agricultural machinery bearing no comparison with that of prewar years.

A fundamental characteristic of the Plan, which earned it the name of "Modernization Plan," was the seeking-out and application of the most modern methods for the purposes of reconstruction and development. French industry and agriculture in 1939 were antiquated, outmoded, had not assimilated the new technologies; the industry and agriculture that would emerge from the Plan would use the techniques of the British (immediately after the war Britain was seen by the French as a country that could serve as a model) and, above all, of the Americans. The action of Jean Monnet, who had spent much of his life in England and America, was decisive in this regard. In short, the aim was not just to expand production, by increasing investment and employment; the overriding objective, one might say, was to push productivity to its maximum. . . .

The biggest problem we had to contend with during the five years that followed the war was the shortage of foreign exchange. France had little to export or, more exactly, it was essential for her to keep almost everything she produced for her own use and consumption. Furthermore, her import needs were immense as regards raw materials, food and capital goods. The supply of gold and foreign exchange she possessed when the war ended was used sparingly, but it was in any case insufficient to meet requirements. External assistance, from America, was essential to see France through those few years. It was generously given. . . .

During the years from 1944 to 1947, that is to say before the Marshall Plan, Jean Monnet played a decisive part in American lending to France thanks to all the friends he had made in the United States during the war and the confidence the Americans placed in him. In the second half of 1944 he had arranged for France's huge purchases from the United States to be effected on the lend-lease basis. In the early part of 1946, in the context of the negotiating assignment on which he was sent to the United States with Léon Blum,[2] he obtained an agreement that tided France over for a while. . . .

This was a substantial amount of aid. It was insufficient, however, to cover the French deficit foreseen for the period of the Plan's execution; but it did buy us the time to wait for an American initiative on the grand scale, which was to come in the form of Marshall Aid. . . .

. . . The active forces of the nation were involved in the design of the Plan itself. On the *Conseil du Plan* [the overall planning board] and the various modernization committees set up for each major area of activity sat representatives of industry, agriculture, the trade unions and the main government service departments. Even though circumstances dictated that they should play an often decisive role in the construction of individual plans and of the overall plan, the decisions produced by this machinery had received acceptance beforehand. All concerned were pledged to take part in carrying them out. It would be true to say that in a country traditionally torn by rival factions, for the first time perhaps in its history, and for a period that was to be relatively brief, a consensus was established to restore life and strength to the nation's economy. The result was spectacular. An impetus was given that was to propel France to a state of prosperity she had never known.

. . . I would stress by way of conclusion that it was to remain a valuable instrument for bringing together the viewpoints of the different social groups and of the government and one which the state could use to maintain or introduce the maximum degree of harmony in the social life of the country.

[2]Prime minister of France from 1936 to 1937, for one month in 1938, and from December 1946 to January 1947.

10

ERNEST BEVIN

The Need for a Western Defensive Alliance

January 22, 1948

British foreign minister Ernest Bevin, in this excerpt from an address to the House of Commons, argued that the free nations of Western Europe had to draw closer together and that "Britain cannot stand outside Europe." This was implicit criticism of Winston Churchill, who opposed close ties between Britain and Europe. Bevin's speech was an important step in his campaign for a mutual defense treaty between France, Italy, Britain, and the Benelux countries—Belgium, the Netherlands, and Luxembourg—to guard against any possible renewed German aggression. The Treaty of Brussels, signed by these six nations in March 1948 to ensure economic collaboration and collective defense, was one of the first practical steps toward a united Western Europe.

Now we have to face a new situation. In this it is impossible to move as quickly as we would wish. We are dealing with nations which are free to take their own decisions. It is easy enough to draw up a blueprint for a united Western Europe and to construct neat-looking plans on paper. While I do not wish to discourage the work done by voluntary political organizations in advocating ambitious schemes of European unity, I must say that it is a much slower and harder job to carry out a practical program which takes into account the realities which face us, and I am afraid that it will have to be done a step at a time.

But surely all these developments which I have been describing, point to the conclusion that the free nations of Western Europe must now draw closely together. How much these countries have in common. Our sacrifices in the war, our hatred of injustice and oppression, our Parliamentary democracy, our striving for economic rights and our conception and love of liberty are common among us all. Our British approach, of which my right hon. Friend the Prime Minister[1]

[1]Clement Attlee, British prime minister, 1945–1951.

Hansard, 5th ser., vol. 446, cols. 395–97.

spoke recently, is based on principles which also appeal deeply to the overwhelming mass of the peoples of Western Europe. I believe the time is ripe for a consolidation of Western Europe.

First in this context we think of the people of France. Like all old friends, we have our differences from time to time, but I doubt whether ever before in our history there has been so much underlying good will and respect between the two peoples as now. We have a firm basis of cooperation in the Treaty of Dunkirk,[2] we are partners in the European recovery program, and I would also remind the House of the useful and practical work being done by the Anglo-French Economic Committee. Through this Committee we have already succeeded in helping one another in our economic difficulties, though at first, to tell the truth, neither of us had very much with which to help the other. But it was useful and the work it did was useful at a very critical moment. We are not now proposing a formal political union with France, as has sometimes been suggested, but we shall maintain the closest possible contact, and work for ever closer unity between the two nations.

The time has come to find ways and means of developing our relations with the Benelux countries. I mean to begin talks with those countries in close accord with our French Ally. I have to inform the House that yesterday our representatives in Brussels, The Hague and Luxembourg were instructed to propose such talks in concert with their French colleagues. I recall that after I signed the Dunkirk Treaty, on my way through Brussels to Moscow, I was asked by a newspaper correspondent, "What about a treaty with other countries including Belgium?" My reply was—I will quote it:

"I hope to sign a similar one with Belgium and with all our good neighbors in the West. The Labour Government will do everything possible to prevent misunderstandings arising from which aggressions might result. You have suffered from two wars; you have twice been occupied in two wars, and England has twice had to fight very hard. Great Britain is still conscious of the great role she has to play. She will do everything possible to prevent a new conflict in the West, whether it will come from Germany or elsewhere."

I hope that treaties will thus be signed with our near neighbors, the Benelux countries, making with our Treaty with France an important nucleus in Western Europe. We have then to go beyond the circle of our immediate neighbors. We shall have to consider the question of

[2]Anglo-French treaty on military assistance signed in March 1947.

associating other historic members of European civilization, including the new Italy, in this great conception. Their eventual participation is of course no less important than that of countries with which, if only for geographical reasons, we must deal first. We are thinking now of Western Europe as a unit. The nations of Western Europe have already shown, at the Paris Conference dealing with the Marshall Plan, their capacity for working together quickly and effectively. That is a good sign for the future. We shall do all we can to foster both the spirit and the machinery of cooperation. In this context I am glad to be able to tell the House that as a practical immediate measure to make our relations with Western Europe closer, His Majesty's Government are proposing to relax the ban on tourist travel. . . .

Our formal relations with the various countries may differ, but between all there should be an effective understanding bound together by common ideals for which the Western Powers have twice in one generation shed their blood. If we are to preserve peace and our own safety at the same time we can only do so by the mobilization of such a moral and material force as will create confidence and energy in the West and inspire respect elsewhere, and this means that Britain cannot stand outside Europe and regard her problems as quite separate from those of her European neighbors.

11

ROBERT MARJOLIN

OEEC's Role: Promoting European Cooperation

April 1948

The Organization for European Economic Cooperation (OEEC) was created in April 1948 because the U.S. government insisted that the sixteen recipient nations of Marshall Plan aid coordinate their planning and economic activities. Robert Marjolin was the OEEC's first secretary-general. In this excerpt from his memoirs, Marjolin described how the

---

Robert Marjolin, *Architect of European Unity: Memoirs, 1911–1986* (London: Weidenfeld and Nicolson, 1989), 191–205.

new institution functioned to maximize the regional benefits of the Marshall Plan and how Europeans and Americans cooperated to make effective use of the aid. He also reflected the uncertainties and doubts that plagued European leaders about whether efforts to achieve close cooperation would prove successful.

In principle the sixteen member countries were equal, but their respective weights were very different. When I put forward a proposal, I had to be sure of the agreement of the British and the French; I also had to be certain that the Americans were not opposed to it. For the small countries, the situation was different. More often than not they had no global view of the problem at issue; on the other hand, they had their individual interests, to which they clung all the closer in that these were more narrowly defined and more concrete. What we had to do, in those first days of European cooperation, was to take initiatives consistent with the views of the big European countries and the United States, and at the same time see that these did not harm the interests of the small countries. All this demanded, in most cases, very lengthy preparations and endless private get-togethers, to explain to each one the real significance and most likely implications of the proposal concerned. It was a job that required infinite patience. Often, a slight adjustment of the text under discussion, which would not alter its sense but would sound better to the ears of those across the table, would be enough to get the decision through. I learned quite quickly this art of negotiation, for which my long stays in England and the United States had prepared me.

But the elation I felt when I was appointed to my new post had another cause. Not only was I happy to be in sole charge of an undertaking, but I had the feeling, subsequently corroborated by the successful outcome, that the OEEC, which was the fruit of the Marshall Plan, would enable Europe and the world to avoid the follies of the interwar years.

. . . The OEEC, along with other international institutions, represented precisely what had been sadly lacking in Europe, and in the whole world, between the two world wars—or between the two phases of the same world war, if one prefers: namely, a dialogue between the great powers so as to ensure continuing peace and erase rapidly the scars left by the war and the Great Depression. This dialogue made it possible to maintain fundamental agreement on objectives and methods among the United States, France and Britain, who would be joined by Germany in the fifties.

The OEEC did not build this agreement from scratch. It already existed, but in a rather unspecific form; it was born of the war and of the awareness that the people in authority in the different countries had gained of the cardinal errors committed in the interwar years. But to be effective, this agreement had to take on a precise form that would respect the vital interests of the different countries and what remained of national ideologies in Europe and the United States; in other words, the agreement of principle had to be converted into a series of major political acts. This was the function of the OEEC and we shall see that it performed that function, if not perfectly, at least highly satisfactorily. . . .

The Secretariat General was mainly Anglo-French, but very soon it found itself working closely with the various European national delegations and with the Americans, and a kind of complicity developed between it and the latter respectively. While the Secretariat General strove to take as objective a view as possible of things, the national delegations themselves toned down or referred back for amendment the instructions they had received from their capitals whenever these contained demands that would have made general agreement impossible.

As to the Americans of the Economic Cooperation Administration (ECA),[1] their major concern was to get the Europeans to come up with sound arguments that would favorably impress the Congress so that it would authorize the appropriations the ECA was requesting for Europe. The strongest argument was that the aid already given had been put to good use and that the recipient countries had made satisfactory progress toward the goals laid down in the European Recovery Program.

There soon came to be a real climate of friendship, compounded of trust and respect for each other's point of view: a communion of minds established itself among the three groups (secretariat, European national delegations, representatives of the ECA). . . .

Our conversations in Paris with the ECA officials were supplemented by frequent trips to Washington where we were able to meet

[1]The Marshall Plan legislation provided for an Economic Cooperation Administration (ECA) to administer the aid program in Europe. Averell Harriman, secretary of commerce in the Truman administration, was appointed special representative of the ECA in Paris to handle day-to-day relations with the Europeans.

members of Congress, who urged us keenly, sometimes excessively so, to make more rapid progress towards European integration. There we also saw Richard Bissell,[2] whose great intellectual abilities and warmth of sentiment towards Europe contributed much to the success of our undertaking. I also had frequent meetings with the head of the ECA, Paul Hoffman,[3] whose authority and prestige helped us greatly in this difficult task. . . .

France and Britain called the tune in the OEEC. . . .

Never in my experience, before and after the Marshall Plan, have I known an international team moved by such an intense desire to accomplish a joint endeavor, the success of which represented at that time a matter of life and death for Europe and for each member country, and to see that it succeeded in conditions such that each participant might derive equal benefit. We were convinced that the different European countries were indissolubly linked in their destinies. Later, the word "cooperation" was somewhat corrupted. But at the time of the Marshall Plan and the OEEC, European cooperation proved to be the key to success, thanks undoubtedly to the circumstances, but also to the exceptional quality of the men who dedicate themselves to this common task. . . .

Our first task was to draw up a consolidated program for all the member countries of the OEEC covering the period from July 1, 1948 to June 30, 1949. The Americans, applying increased pressure to make Europe behave as much as possible like a unit, declared that the responsibility of coordinating and integrating the individual country programs should fall to the OEEC.

Each of these programs ultimately represented a request for aid. . . .

. . . Averell Harriman announced to the OEEC Council that the ECA would like the OEEC, in establishing the economic recovery program for 1948–9, to indicate how, in its opinion, American aid should be apportioned among the different countries and the uses to which it should be put by each.

What the Americans were asking of us was a recommendation; they reserved the final decision for themselves, of course. Experience showed that they followed the European recommendations to the letter in 1948–9 and, with only a comparatively minor adjustment, in 1949–50. The Americans' essential motivation was to induce maximum unity among the European countries. A secondary consideration, but

[2]Assistant deputy administrator of the ECA.
[3]President of the Studebaker Company; chosen to be the administrator of the ECA.

influential nonetheless, was their wish not to be involved in bilateral horse-trading with each of the European countries. . . .

The first division of U.S. aid had made the Europeans euphoric. The Americans now wanted us to outline for them the prospect of a Europe that would quite soon be able to do without their assistance. At the outset of the work that culminated in the European Recovery Program a time limit of four years had been set, a magic figure that rested on no measurable reality. It represented no more than a vague aspiration shared by the Americans and the Europeans; but there had to be a figure, preferably a very low one, to give Congress and the American people the feeling that Europe was not a bottomless receptacle. This, at least, was the conviction of the ECA. On July 25, 1948 Paul Hoffman, speaking before the OEEC Council, called for a plan of action of which the goal would be Europe's complete and definitive recovery at the latest by June 30, 1952, when American aid would cease. . . .

Today, as we approach the end of the 20th century, what often remains in the minds of those who lived through the postwar period is the memory of Europe's renascent prosperity and of its prodigious economic expansion over twenty-five years. My testimony is designed, among other things, to dispel the belief that from the very outset we were possessed of a fine certitude, an indomitable faith in the future, an unshakeable optimism. On the contrary, what remains branded on my memory is the doubts, the dread of the morrow, the fear of failing, the concern with continually adjusting our action in the light of experience—and I can never say it enough—having the grievous reminders of the interwar years as a constant warning.

12

JEAN MONNET

Europe Must Build "a True Western Federation"

April 18, 1948

While in the United States negotiating to buy wheat for France, Monnet, head of the French economic plan (the Monnet Plan), wrote to French foreign minister Robert Schuman describing the American mood, gleaned from his contacts with Washington friends and officials. Monnet argued that Europe must build a Western federation in order to avoid another war. Implicit in his letter, excerpted here, was the fear of renewed German aggression and increased political subversion from the Soviet Union and communism. Monnet stressed that a federation would eliminate Europe's dependence on the United States for funds and security and thus help Europe resist domination by that nation. This letter reflects his hope that one day Europe would be treated as an equal partner by the United States.

During my stay here, I saw on intimate terms a lot of people I have known for a long time. I will describe everything in detail to you in Paris. Of course, I was in daily contact with Bonnet,[1] to whom I reported all of the conversations I had. You know America well enough to understand that these were amicable, unofficial conversations which sprang, quite obviously, from the friendly, often close personal relationships I have had here for a long time.

I am very content with my trip. After being away for two years, my impressions are more vivid than they would have been had I stayed in constant touch with things here. The changes have struck me more forcefully; then again, my sense of what constitutes the essential nature of American life has been strengthened. This country is constantly energized by a dynamic force that arises out of the character of each individual. America is moving forward, but it is neither reactionary

[1]Henri Bonnet, French ambassador to the United States, 1944–1955.

Jean Monnet–Robert Schuman Correspondance, 1947–1953 (Lausanne: Fondation Jean Monnet pour l'Europe, 1986), 35–38. Translated by Paul Hurwit.

nor imperialist. It does not *want* war, but will wage war if necessary. Its resolve on this point is quite strong. But it's not a blind determination. I will explain to you the transformation that has occurred here over the last few weeks: The Americans began by preparing for war, they have now reached the stage where they are preparing to stop the war—and now the idea of a possible détente is making itself felt. In any event, the current state of their leaders' minds is reflected by this watchword: firm resolve, but prudence.

I prefer reporting to you verbally my observations and my opinion regarding this aspect of the American attitude and what we can expect from it.

But we must realize, as I said before, that America is driven primarily by a desire *for action*—that is, action at home—and also in the other countries. For America, action today means preventing war, helping Western Europe to rebuild, and clearing the way for stopping Russian expansion. They are going to undertake a major effort to accomplish these things. They realize perfectly well that the financial side of the undertaking is formidable. The Marshall Plan and the military funding, which are only at the beginning stages, will represent an enormous burden; inflation is a certainty, as are tax increases. While manifesting the desire to make the effort, Congress will approve the funding allocations only after strenuous debate. [Paul] Hoffman will have a difficult job when he appears before Congress next February to ask for approval of the funds for the second year of the Marshall Plan. He is already thinking about it and preparing for it.

In the mind of everyone here, the European effort must match the American one—first of all, a production campaign, but also an effort of another kind. They will support these efforts in all sorts of ways and with determination. Yet we must recognize that both the American leaders and public opinion expect much from us. We will be cruelly deceived if we believe that the Marshall funds will be allocated far into the future if Europe cannot quickly demonstrate strengthened, modernized production capabilities.

I cannot help being forcefully struck by the nature of the relations that may be formed between this great country and the European nations if the latter retain their present forms and current attitudes. In my view, Europe cannot remain almost exclusively "dependent" on American funding for its output, and on American strength for its security, without the emergence of adverse repercussions here and in Europe.

All of my thoughts and observations are leading me to one conclusion, which has now become my deepest conviction: The effort made by the countries of Western Europe to be able to confront current circumstances, the danger that threatens us, and the American enterprise must become a truly European effort, which only the existence of a Western *Federation* can bring to fruition. I am well aware of all of the difficulties such a prospect entails, but my belief is that only an undertaking of this kind will enable us to save ourselves, to keep our identity, and to help at the fundamental level to avoid war.

In this regard, when he was in Washington [Paul-Henri] Spaak told me that he had suggested me as president of the Executive Committee of the Sixteen.[2] I told him I was not interested. First, because the implementation of the [Monnet] Plan in France has now become possible because of the Marshall funds, and because rapid implementation has become still more urgent for the reasons I gave earlier. In addition, I believe that the members of the Executive Committee of the Sixteen should be Cripps,[3] [René] Mayer, and their colleagues. I added that the only job to which I would be prepared to devote myself outside of the Plan would be to help to build a true Western Federation.

[2]The Executive Committee of the Organization for European Economic Cooperation (OEEC).

[3]Sir Stafford Cripps, British finance minister, 1947–1950.

13

JEAN MONNET

"I Saw Our Policy towards Germany Beginning to Slip Back into Its Old Ways"

April 1948

This excerpt from Monnet's memoirs reflects his realization that Germany's rapidly recovering economy would absorb all the German coke produced in the Ruhr area and prevent French steel production from meeting the Monnet Plan's targets, a key to French reconstruction. He worried, too, about the growing opposition from private interests and the public to Germany's inevitable rehabilitation.

Jean Monnet, *Memoirs* (Garden City, N.Y.: Doubleday, 1978), 274.

The Marshall Plan's production targets aimed at restoring the German economy, like that of Europe as a whole, by 1952—but without allowing it once again to become autarkic.[1] In August 1947, in some Allied documents which Marjolin had passed to me, I found some disturbing facts. The German steel industry would soon be absorbing all the coke produced in the Ruhr, with the result that steel production in France and the rest of Europe would have to be limited. In these circumstances, it was hard to see how Europe's global targets could be attained. Economically and politically, this would be unacceptable; and I saw no solution except to propose linking the growth of German steel production to an increase in Ruhr coke exports, by means of some sophisticated sliding scale. Only in this way could we maintain France's steel production targets, which were the key to the whole French Plan.

I had few illusions about the effectiveness of such expedients; and it was with growing anxiety that I saw our policy towards Germany beginning to slip back into its old ways. True, in 1948 we were no longer demanding that the former *Reich* be politically dismembered; but, in varying degrees, all shades of public opinion, all public authorities, and all private interests in France were supporting our diplomatic rearguard action against Germany's inevitable rehabilitation.

[1]The condition of self-sufficiency, especially economic, as applied to a state.

14

PAUL-HENRI SPAAK

The Congress of Europe

May 7–11, 1948

In this excerpt from his memoirs, Belgian prime minister Paul-Henri Spaak described how Churchill's Zurich speech in 1946 had motivated the champions of European unity to join forces and organize the Congress of Europe in 1948. More than fifteen hundred influential Euro-

Paul-Henri Spaak, *The Continuing Battle: Memoirs of a European, 1936–1966* (Boston: Little, Brown, 1971), 199–205.

peans—former heads of state such as Winston Churchill and Léon Blum, Paul van Zeeland, and other dignitaries, and seven hundred parliamentary deputies from every free country in Europe—met in The Hague to plan a strategy for European unity. Sharp differences punctuated their debates, especially between the "unionists," who advocated intergovernmental cooperation personified by Churchill, and the "federalists," who advocated the "supranationalism" espoused by Altiero Spinelli and his followers. Both sides agreed that European integration was desirable and that an organization with a parliamentary body had to be established. Their deliberations led to the creation of the Council of Europe in 1949, an intergovernmental body located in Strasbourg and designed to work for greater economic and political union.

In the years that followed the end of the Second World War, when it became clear that there was no prospect of continued cooperation with the USSR and that it was essential to organize Western solidarity, the idea of a united Europe was revived and pursued with more vigor than at any time in the past. The situation had been transformed by a new element: the idea was now being championed and publicized by important statesmen. Thanks to them, the transformation of Europe ceased to be an abstract notion and became a topical political issue.

Winston Churchill, whose Fulton speech [Document 4] had shaken the Atlantic world, created a fresh stir in Europe with an address in Zurich on 19 September 1946 [Document 5]. Although defeated in the previous year's general elections, he still enjoyed tremendous prestige and undeniable authority throughout the democratic world. His unexpected move caused a considerable stir. The Zurich speech was beautiful: it followed the true Churchillian tradition, being serious, dramatic and full of passion, and it combined poetical language with an acute awareness of the needs of the moment. He justified his vision of the future by his interpretation of the events of the day. When one remembers that Churchill made his speech a mere eighteen months after the end of hostilities, one can but feel boundless admiration for the man; although already old, he did not flinch from new and tough battles.

The Zurich speech galvanized all those who believed in the need for a new Europe. By making that speech, Churchill became one of the leading pioneers of European unity. And yet the speech was to become the root cause of a grave misunderstanding, for it contained an ambiguity which no one noticed at the time. . . .

Though even on a careful reading his Zurich address seems clear, Churchill, in referring to Europe in some splendid passages, failed to define what exactly he meant by Europe in geographical terms. At the time, he appeared to include Great Britain in Europe, but in fact this was not the case. The united Europe which Churchill advocated was a continental Europe, of which France and Germany were to be the joint leaders; Great Britain, the Commonwealth, the United States and, if possible, the USSR, were to befriend and support it.

Churchill wanted Britain to promote the creation of a united Europe, but he did not want Britain to be part of it. . . .

But whatever may have been the true sense of Churchill's speech at Zurich, the impulse had been given. All the unofficial movements which championed the cause of European unity joined forces in organizing a great congress to voice their demands. It was held at The Hague from 7 to 11 May 1948, and was to become an historic landmark in the annals of Europe. A huge number of delegates attended—more than 1,200. Among those present were Churchill, representing Britain; Ramadier and Reynaud[1] representing France; and van Zeeland[2] for Belgium. Also present were two men who were as yet little known but who were soon to play a major role: [Konrad] Adenauer and [Alcide] De Gasperi. . . .

The congress duly ended with a vote on three resolutions dealing, respectively, with cultural, economic and political affairs.

The first called for the establishment of a European cultural center: this was set up within a matter of years. The second proclaimed a set of principles, most of which are now embodied in the Treaty of Rome. The third urged that a European parliamentary assembly be convened immediately.

The resolutions adopted at The Hague, bold though they were, were evidently well thought out, since all of them—and this is rare where congress resolutions are concerned—were to be carried into effect within a few years.

The most urgent task—and the first that was in fact tackled because it was also the easiest and most spectacular—was the establishment of a European Assembly. . . .

[1]Paul Ramadier, French prime minister, January–November 1947; defense minister, 1948–1949. Paul Reynaud, French prime minister, March–June, 1940; finance and economic affairs minister, 1948.

[2]Paul van Zeeland, Belgian prime minister, 1935–1937; foreign affairs minister in several cabinets.

The communiqué published at the end of the meeting announced that agreement had been reached on the establishment of a Council of Europe which would consist of a Ministerial Council and a Consultative Assembly. The Council would deliberate in private and its decisions would, alas, be subject to the rule of unanimity, while the Assembly's meetings would be public. Italy was to be invited to join. At Bevin's suggestion, Strasbourg was chosen as the seat of the new organization. This border town, which had so often in history been the object of Franco-German rivalry, was selected as a symbol of cooperation and friendship.

The treaty establishing the Council of Europe was signed in London on 5 May 1949 by representatives of the five Powers which had taken part in the negotiations, plus the three Scandinavian countries, Italy and the Republic of Ireland. The Treaty of London incorporated the main points on which the Five had agreed. Its preamble stressed the need for international cooperation for the maintenance of peace and reaffirmed a number of moral and political principles fundamental to European civilization, as well as the need for economic cooperation as a means of encouraging social progress.

15

ALCIDE DE GASPERI

The Approach toward the Political and Economic Union of Europe Must Be Gradual, "Genuine, and Lasting"

February 20, 1950

In a reply to federalist arguments, excerpted here, Alcide De Gasperi, prime minister of Italy and leader of the Christian Democratic party, declared that political union and economic and commercial integration were "interdependent processes and react upon each other."

"L'unione europea," *Il Popolo*, February 20, 1950, in *Documents on the History of European Integration*, ed. Walter Lipgens and Wilfried Loth (Berlin: Walter de Gruyter, 1988), 3:250–51.

There are some who complain of a certain slowness, an unduly gradual approach towards the economic integration and political unification of Europe. But a reasonable degree of gradualness should inspire confidence in our friends and not distrust.

We have to work for a political and economic union that will be genuine and lasting, and this requires a detailed exchange of ideas and proposals and the careful examination of mutual concessions.

The fact that we have been stimulated to make concessions in such delicate matters as national economic interests, which in the past have been so jealously watched over, shows how strong is the impulse and how convinced we are of the need for European unity. . . .

Our American friends must not consider European union as a new creation—one of the many international institutions that spring up at particular historical moments on the initiative of men of good will who desire to consolidate peace, harmonize discordant views and eliminate disputes. Although such institutions are new, they are indispensable and can easily be constructed in perfect accordance with the schemes of their inventors.

We must, as we have made clear internationally, continue towards integration in multiple directions. We must, for instance, ensure the liberalization of movement not only of capital but of human beings: otherwise we cannot solve the problem of unemployment, which at present weighs so heavily on Italy. Without the free movement of labor the general problem of the liberalization of trade will not be solved but aggravated. And we must see to the integration of economic and financial policy and international political cooperation. . . .

All these problems should be dealt with simultaneously and, I repeat, gradually, if the economies that are not prostrate as a result of the war are to be enabled to return to a normal state. Political union and economic and commercial integration are interdependent processes and react upon each other.

2

French-German Rapprochement

16

JEAN MONNET

"France's Continued Recovery Will Come to a Halt Unless We Rapidly Solve the Problem of German Industrial Production and Its Competitive Capacity"

May 3, 1950

In a memorandum to French foreign minister Robert Schuman, partially quoted in his Memoirs, *Monnet explained why his government needed to take immediate action to deal with Germany's competitive capacity. Because French economic recovery depended on access to German resources, Monnet had proposed to Schuman on April 28 that France and Germany pool their coal and steel industries under joint management of a supranational authority.*

In the confused state of Franco-German relations, the neurosis of the vanquished seemed to be shifting to the victor: France was beginning to feel inferior again as she realized that attempts to limit Germany's dynamism were bound to fail.

Jean Monnet, *Memoirs* (Garden City, N.Y.: Doubleday, 1978), 292–93; text of memorandum in *Un changement d'espérance: La Déclaration du 9 mai 1950, Jean Monnet–Robert Schuman*, ed. Henri Rieben et al. (Lausanne: Fondation Jean Monnet pour l'Europe, Centre de recherches européennes, 2000), 89–97.

> France's continued recovery will come to a halt unless we rapidly solve the problem of German industrial production and its competitive capacity.
>
> The basis of the superiority which French industrialists traditionally recognize in Germany is her ability to produce steel at a price that France cannot match. From this they conclude that the whole of French production is similarly handicapped.
>
> Already, Germany is seeking to increase her production from eleven to fourteen million metric tons. We shall refuse, but the Americans will insist. Finally, we shall state our reservations, but we shall give in. At the same time, French production is leveling off or even falling.
>
> Merely to state these facts makes it unnecessary to describe what the results will be: Germany expanding; German dumping on export markets; a call for the protection of French industry; an end to trade liberalization; the re-establishment of prewar cartels; perhaps, Eastward outlets for German expansion, a prelude to political agreements; and France back in the old rut of limited, protected production.

From my vantage-point at the Planning Commissariat, I could clearly detect the first signs of such a retreat on the part of France. . . . If only the French could lose their fear of German industrial domination, then the greatest obstacle to a united Europe would be removed. A solution which would put French industry on the same footing as German industry, while freeing the latter from the discrimination born of defeat—that would restore the economic and political preconditions for the mutual understanding so vital to Europe as a whole. It could, in fact, become the germ of European unity.

17

ROBERT SCHUMAN

The Schuman Declaration

May 9, 1950

French foreign minister Robert Schuman announced this bold initiative, designed by Jean Monnet, to the public at a crowded press conference in Paris on May 9, 1950. The Schuman Declaration led to the treaty creating the European Coal and Steel Community (ECSC), the first concrete step taken to achieve Franco-German rapprochement.

World peace cannot be safeguarded without the making of creative efforts proportionate to the dangers which threaten it.

The contribution which an organized and living Europe can bring to civilization is indispensable to the maintenance of peaceful relations. In taking upon herself for more than 20 years the role of champion of a united Europe, France has always had as her essential aim the service of peace. A united Europe was not achieved and we had war.

Europe will not be made all at once, or according to a single plan. It will be built through concrete achievements which first create a *de facto* solidarity. The coming together of the nations of Europe requires the elimination of the age-old opposition of France and Germany. Any action taken must in the first place concern these two countries.

With this aim in view, the French Government proposes that action be taken immediately on one limited but decisive point. It proposes that Franco-German production of coal and steel as a whole be placed under a common High Authority, within the framework of an organization open to the participation of the other countries of Europe.

The pooling of coal and steel production should immediately provide for the setting up of common foundations for economic development as a first step in the federation of Europe, and will change the

Schuman Declaration available at http://www.europa.eu/abc/symbols/9-may/decl_en.htm; also available with commentary at http://www.aei.pitt.edu/5877/; also in *Europe—A Fresh Start: The Schuman Declaration, 1950–90* (Luxembourg: Office for Official Publications of the European Communities, 1990), 44–46.

destinies of those regions which have long been devoted to the manufacture of munitions of war, of which they have been the most constant victims.

The solidarity in production thus established will make it plain that any war between France and Germany becomes not merely unthinkable, but materially impossible. The setting up of this powerful productive unit, open to all countries willing to take part and bound ultimately to provide all the member countries with the basic elements of industrial production on the same terms, will lay a true foundation for their economic unification.

This production will be offered to the world as a whole without distinction or exception, with the aim of contributing to raising living standards and to promoting peaceful achievements.

In this way, there will be realized simply and speedily that fusion of interests which is indispensable to the establishment of a common economic system; it may be the leaven from which may grow a wider and deeper community between countries long opposed to one another by sanguinary divisions.

By pooling basic production and by instituting a new High Authority, whose decisions will bind France, Germany and other member countries, this proposal will lead to the realization of the first concrete foundation of a European federation indispensable to the preservation of peace.

To promote the realization of the objectives defined, the French Government is ready to open negotiations on the following bases:

The task with which this common High Authority will be charged will be that of securing in the shortest possible time the modernization of production and the improvement of its quality; the supply of coal and steel on identical terms to the French and German markets, as well as to the markets of other member countries; the development in common of exports to other countries; the equalization and improvement of the living conditions of workers in these industries.

To achieve these objectives, starting from the very different conditions in which the production of member countries is at present situated, it is proposed that certain transitional measures should be instituted, such as the application of a production and investment plan, the establishment of compensating machinery for equating prices, and the creation of a restructuring fund to facilitate the rationalization of production. The movement of coal and steel between member countries will immediately be freed from all customs duty, and will not be affected by differential transport rates. Conditions will gradually be created which will spontaneously provide for the more national distribution of production at the highest level of productivity.

In contrast to international cartels, which tend to impose restrictive practices on distribution and the exploitation of national markets, and to maintain high profits, the organization will ensure the fusion of markets and the expansion of production.

The essential principles and undertakings defined above will be the subject of a treaty signed between the States and submitted for the ratification of their parliaments. The negotiations required to settle details of application will be undertaken with the help of an arbitrator appointed by common agreement. He will be entrusted with the task of seeing that the agreements reached conform with the principles laid down, and, in the event of a deadlock, he will decide what solution is to be adopted. The common High Authority entrusted with the management of the scheme will be composed of independent persons appointed by the governments, giving equal representation. A chairman will be chosen by common agreement between the governments. The Authority's decisions will be enforceable in France, Germany and other member countries. Appropriate measures will be provided for means of appeal against the decisions of the Authority.

A representative of the United Nations will be accredited to the Authority, and will be instructed to make a public report to the United Nations twice yearly, giving an account of the working of the new organization, particularly as concerns the safeguarding of its specific objectives.

The institution of the High Authority will in no way prejudge the methods of ownership of enterprises. In the exercise of its functions, the common High Authority will take into account the powers conferred upon the International Ruhr Authority and the obligations of all kinds imposed upon Germany, so long as these remain in force.

18

JOHN FOSTER DULLES

The Schuman Plan's "Conception Is Brilliantly Creative"

May 10, 1950

John Foster Dulles, leading Republican consultant to U.S. secretary of state Dean Acheson, cabled the secretary after hearing Schuman's proposals. Acheson's initial reaction to the plan was negative, but Dulles's enthusiastic support for it and indication it would receive bipartisan support helped change his mind. Acheson praised the plan in his 1969 book Present at the Creation *and wrote, "The genius of the Schuman-Monnet plan lay in its practical, commonsense approach, its avoidance of limitations upon sovereignty, and touchy political problems. What could be more earthy than coal and steel, or more desirable than pooling a common direction of France and Germany's coal and steel industries?"*

I have just read the text of Schuman's statement regarding new political authority to unify and administer German-French coal and steel resources. While obviously many details [are] lacking [that are] necessary for final judgment, it is my initial impression that the conception is brilliantly creative and could go far to solve the most dangerous problem of our time, namely the relationship of Germany's industrial power to France and the West. This proposal is along lines which Secretary Marshall and I thought about in Moscow in 1947 but which we did not believe the French would ever accept.

Foreign Relations of the United States, 1950, III, 695–97. See Dean Acheson, *Present at the Creation: My Years in the State Department* (New York: W. W. Norton, 1969), 383–84.

19

JEAN MONNET

Meeting with Adenauer: Sharing Identical Views

May 23, 1950

Monnet traveled to Bonn to explain the details of the Schuman proposals personally to West German chancellor Konrad Adenauer, whom he had never met. The French summary of the meeting excerpted here indicated that the two leaders discovered they shared the same goals for Europe. Herbert Blankenhorn, Germany's ambassador in Paris and Adenauer's closest adviser, also summarized the meeting. He stressed that the two leaders agreed the Schuman Plan was "above all a moral matter" and that the French and West German statesmen were "obligated by an inner responsibility to their people to execute this plan." Adenauer had remarked that "if fear were to be overcome, then Europe like a recovering ill person would again find strength."

Mr. Monnet gave to the Chancellor an account of the origins, objectives, and details of the Schuman Plan. On this occasion, he made it known that this plan, which had been formulated in close cooperation with Messrs. [Robert] Schuman and [Georges] Bidault, had gained the approval of the entire French Government. He stated again that the other initiatives that had been taken with a view toward creating a European union, e.g., OEEC, Organization of Strasbourg, had not made conclusive progress.

This situation threatened to inspire a stinging disappointment in public sentiment. It was necessary to climb out of this stagnation and move forward. The defect of the previous undertakings had been to seek to establish a federation of nationally sovereign States. To the

---

Jean Monnet Archives, Fondation Jean Monnet pour l'Europe, Lausanne, AMG 2/3/11. Translated by Paul Hurwit. For Blankenhorn's May 24, 1950, summary, see *Atken zur Auswärtigen Politik der Bundesrepublik Deutschland*, ed. Hans-Peter Schwartz (Munich: R. Oldenbourg Verlag, 1997), 154–59. Segment quoted above translated by Harold Radday.

contrary, it was essential to create a supranational authority for which the various national governments would be the enforcement agents, each within its own sphere of authority. Another defect of the undertakings attempted to date lay in the failure to specify a concrete mission. The States would agree to relinquish a part of their sovereign power only for a common good, for a specific task.

The French Government had opined that this task was to be sought in the sphere of Franco-German relations, which represented the nerve center of the situation in Western Europe. By building these relations on a new foundation, it would be possible to remove the fear of war and, as Roosevelt once asserted, "the real danger is the fear of danger." The French Government had also felt that, within the context of Franco-German relations, coal and steel played a crucial role because they impinged on the security question and because they had supplied the means for triggering past conflicts. In public opinion these heavy industries were linked to the idea of warfare. By diverting them toward a common good it would be possible to transform the psychological climate completely.

On this subject, Mr. Monnet underscored the fact that, if Europe no longer wasted its energies on internal strife, it could attain an especially high standard of living. It would assume once again the leadership role which, from an intellectual perspective and the standpoint of civilization, it had once played in the world and which it must play again. It enjoyed a diversity that constituted its wealth and that was lacking in America. If it regained its prosperity, it could for that reason exercise an influence on the progress of America itself.

Accordingly, the inspiration for the French proposal was basically political in nature. It even had what could be called a moral aspect. Essentially, it was aimed at a very simple objective which our government would attempt to achieve without worrying initially about technical difficulties.

There was nothing in our initiative that had not been set forth in Mr. Schuman's declaration of May 9, which was given to the Chancellor. In speaking to the Chancellor, Mr. Monnet used the language he had spoken before the High Commission and, previously, with the English and the Benelux countries. In certain respects, the English had proved somewhat reticent, a completely understandable posture since they had to take their Empire into account and were troubled about their economic situation. There was no reason to be worried about it, however. The English had the great characteristic of being realists; if the undertaking succeeded, the English would certainly become its adherents. The Benelux representatives had shown themselves to be favorable to it. Italy had pressed to be associated with it.

In general, the Schuman Proposal had resonated deeply with public opinion. It had inspired so strong and sincere an approval that the peoples would no longer accept any disappointed expectations. They would rise above the technical problems and would urge their governments to arrive at a successful conclusion. It was necessary to take advantage of this circumstance, to keep from wasting time, and to take action as soon as possible.

Such action had to take the form of negotiations leading to an overarching treaty creating the supranational authority. Once this entity was instituted, the solution to the technical problems would be addressed. As a specialist in technical matters, Mr. Monnet knew by experience that these problems could always be solved, starting at the moment when they were viewed from the vantage point of a great idea.

Mr. Monnet was to return to Paris. The next day, he was to have new discussions with the Benelux representatives. Quite probably, the latter would join in our initiative. At that time, we could in all likelihood expect a communiqué announcing that the French, German, and Benelux governments, and possibly also the British and Italian governments, had approved the immediate opening of negotiations based on the French memorandum of May 19, whose terms they said they had accepted. The Federal Government [West Germany] would have to name a negotiator, the choice of whom took on a great importance, according to Mr. Monnet. This choice should not settle on a technical expert, a specialist who would emphasize a particular difficulty; nor should it be a politician who would be driven by party concerns. The negotiator should be an independent, disinterested person. This German representative would negotiate on the basis of complete equality, so as to guarantee that the prospective treaty, which would be the starting point for a new era in European history, would appear in everyone's eyes as the product of unforced debates. The Federal Government would have to ask the High Commission for authorization to send this negotiator to Paris, just as Mr. Monnet had received notice to talk this afternoon with the Chancellor. This request would encounter no obstacle, however. After the meeting that had taken place during the morning at Petersberg, Mr. Monnet could, moreover, tell the Chancellor that the High Commission would not ask that the German negotiator be assisted by an observer.

Mr. Clappier[1] took the floor to state confidentially to Mr. Adenauer that Mr. Schuman had already named Mr. Monnet as negotiator. He also reviewed the terms set forth in the Declaration of May 9, in order to underscore the fact that, while the negotiations would unfold with complete equality among the parties, each partner would nevertheless participate under the status it currently held. In other words, the Federal Government would not in consequence be released from its obligations.

In reply to Mr. Monnet, Mr. Adenauer asserted that he himself was not a technical expert, and that he was not totally a politician, either. For his part, he, too, viewed this undertaking in the loftiest terms and as a moral endeavor. The various governments concerned should be concerned not so much with the technical responsibilities they were to assume on behalf of their peoples, as with their moral duty, given the enormous hopes this proposal had awakened. The Chancellor and his government would not focus on secondary matters, on narrow viewpoints, on details. The reception in Germany had been enthusiastic. While criticisms had been leveled by the Social Democrats, they should not be taken too seriously. In Germany, when a head of government approves an initiative 100%, the opposition must back off by at least 20%. Germany was prepared to carry out the French proposal. The Chancellor agreed to the communiqué he had been given by Mr. Monnet, which was to be published at the moment when negotiations would begin in Paris. The text was left with him, it being understood that it would remain secret until the time of its publication. Mr. Adenauer maintained that he was especially well-disposed toward our initiative because he himself had been preoccupied with this matter for 25 years. If the parties concerned were able to reach a satisfactory solution to the coal and steel problems, the atmosphere of fear that still prevailed would dissipate, and a strong foundation would be in place for the building of Europe.

The Chancellor wanted to state that, by joining in the proposed undertaking, his government and his nation had no ulterior motive inspired by a desire for hegemony. Since 1933 in particular, history had demonstrated the uselessness of such views. Germany, like Europe, was now being assailed by direct pressures from the East, from Asia, and it knew quite well that its destiny was linked to that of Western Europe.

[1]Bernard Clappier, Schuman's principal adviser.

Mr. Monnet repeated that Europe had a moral contribution to make to world progress. If Europe succeeded in tearing the causes of war out of its bosom, it would bestow on the world this spiritual gift, which rivalries and opposition between nationalisms was still making impossible.

The Chancellor hoped that England would grasp the nature of its role in Europe. In all honesty, he had no doubt about it, but the English are people who need a little time. Italy would prove to be well-disposed, as would the Benelux countries. The Federal Government was facing one problem: finding its own Mr. Monnet, since Germany had few eminent men like him. . . .

Mr. Monnet asserted that it was not so much competence that mattered. With all political problems, the approach was the hard part. The question now before Europe had to be addressed by action that would lead to a common good. It was necessary for the Chancellor to take matters into his own hands, as Mr. Schuman was doing in Paris, and for his representative to report directly to him.

. . . In closing, the Chancellor stated that he considered the implementation of the French proposal to be the most important mission falling to him. If he succeeded in reaching the proper resolution, he would feel that he had not wasted his life.

Mr. Monnet replied that this initiative could, in fact, create the psychological conditions that would help to eliminate war once and for all.

The discussion took place in an extremely cordial atmosphere. It obviously allowed a climate of confidence to take root between the two men. As he accompanied Mr. Monnet to the door, the Chancellor told him that he was delighted to think that their conversation would continue over dinner, when they would meet again.

. . . Mr. Jean Monnet and the Chancellor found that, on these subjects, they shared entirely identical views, and in particular, on the advantage to be gained by rapid implementation of this undertaking.

20

PAUL-HENRI SPAAK

Enthusiastic Support for the Schuman Plan

August 1950

Spaak applauded the courage of Schuman and Monnet in proposing that German and French coal and steel production be placed under a joint authority with supranational powers. In this excerpt from his memoirs, he underlined the difference between the pioneers who pursued European unity through the functional approach and those who advocated the intergovernmental approach of the Council of Europe.

On 9 May 1950, at the Quai d'Orsay, Robert Schuman gave a press conference at which he outlined the plan that was to constitute the basis of the European Coal and Steel Community. That plan had been drawn up by Jean Monnet. In saying this I do not in the least wish to detract from the part played by Robert Schuman. His contribution—and it was essential—was to have accepted political responsibility for Monnet's ideas.

I met Jean Monnet for the first time in Washington in 1941 and remember the occasion very clearly for two reasons: first, because of what he said to me and, second—dare I admit it?—because of the excellent dinner he offered me: chocolate profiteroles—creamy and light, rounded off a splendid meal prepared by his French chef. The dinner made an agreeable contrast with the austerity of British cooking to which I was subjected at that time.

Having tasted these material delights, we went for a walk which took us along a route from which we were able to admire the panorama of Washington. We spoke of the post-war period, of what would have to be done to safeguard peace and Europe's future. Monnet gave me an account of the underlying philosophy, and explained the rough outlines of what later became known as the Schuman Plan.

It is this continuity of thought, this perseverance in pursuing his

---

Paul-Henri Spaak, *The Continuing Battle: Memoirs of a European, 1936–1966* (Boston: Little, Brown, 1971), 213–15.

ideas, that I feel is Jean Monnet's most characteristic trait. Like Robert Schuman, he is a man of modest bearing, in fact he even seems shy. But though Monnet may not be an impressive public speaker, in his day-to-day work he is incomparable and the strength of his convictions is unequaled. I have seen him deal with individuals as different from one another as one could wish to find: captains of industry, government leaders, trade union militants, Members of Parliament of every political hue. By the time Jean Monnet had finished with them, they were all convinced of the rightness of his views. Thus he made converts one by one.

In the immediate post-war years, he played a crucial part in the efforts to create a United Europe. We all looked up to him as our master and relied on him for advice. Nothing was done without him in this connection at that time. His untiring and selfless efforts earned him our devotion, respect and admiration.

In the spring of 1950, Robert Schuman and Jean Monnet, realizing that the endless discussions in Strasbourg were a sheer waste of time and that there was no chance of a federal solution ever being adopted, decided to approach the problems of European unity from another angle. They became advocates of the functional approach. Robert Schuman declared: "Europe will not be created all at once, nor will it be a unitary structure. Europe will be the result of specific measures. To begin with, our solidarity will take the shape of practical ties."

There was, however, a great deal of courage behind this apparent moderation. The French Government was in fact proposing that the whole of French and German coal and steel production should be placed under a joint authority which would enjoy supranational powers and would "create the first practical basis for a European federation, essential if peace is to be preserved."

The final goal had thus not been forgotten. Though the idea was to approach it stage by stage, the supranational principle was to be applied from the outset. For my own part, I accepted this proposal enthusiastically. . . .

On 13 August 1950, Robert Schuman defended his plan before the Consultative Assembly in Strasbourg[1] on behalf of the Ministerial Council as well as in his own name. He gave numerous technical details to justify the plan and, on the most crucial matter of all—that of the supranational character of its institutions—he declared:

[1]Council of Europe deliberations.

I accept a renunciation of sovereign rights not for its own sake, not as an end in itself, but as a necessity, as the only means at our disposal to overcome national selfishness, the enmities and narrow-minded prejudices which are ruining us.

He concluded by saying:

We do not think we are being presumptuous in claiming that if our proposal, which you have accepted, becomes a reality in the form in which it has been submitted to and accepted by you, forces will have been set free whose potential cannot as yet be measured. One thing, however, is certain: they will promote rapid and complete economic and political unification of Europe.

The speech led to prolonged discussion which showed that the functional approach was bound to give rise to difficulties just as hard to overcome as those of the legislative approach.

21

JEAN MONNET

"The Schuman Proposals Are Revolutionary"

August 1950

British leaders refused to participate in the Schuman Plan because they firmly opposed delegating any power to a supranational authority in Europe. They also feared that changing their relations with European powers might diminish their role as the nerve center of the Commonwealth. In Strasbourg, Monnet circulated a letter, written in English, countering British opposition to the Schuman Plan. This excerpt from his Memoirs *quoted part of the letter and places it in context. The French decision to work with the Germans, as opposed to the British, their original choice, was an important step in the evolution of the integration process. In the second excerpt from his* Memoirs, *Monnet quoted from his 1953 speech to the ECSC's Common Assembly. There he underscored*

Jean Monnet, *Memoirs* (Garden City, N.Y.: Doubleday, 1978), 316, 392–93.

the revolutionary nature of the "ECSC's method" because of his core belief that international institutions transform relationships between peoples.

> The Schuman proposals are revolutionary or they are nothing.... Cooperation between nations, while essential, cannot alone meet our problem. What must be sought is a fusion of the interests of the European peoples and not merely another effort to maintain an equilibrium of those interests through additional machinery for negotiation....
>
> The Schuman proposals provide a basis for the building of a new Europe through the concrete achievement of a supranational regime within a limited but controlling area of economic effort.... The indispensable first principle of these proposals is the abnegation of sovereignty in a limited but decisive field and..., in my view, any plan which does not involve this indispensable first principle can make no useful contribution to the solution of the grave problems that face us.

Later, Macmillan came round to this point of view. In the meantime, I wanted him not to create too much confusion. I added:

> I know the British people well enough to be confident that they will never oppose a progressive measure for the benefit of all Europe even though their special problems may for the moment prevent their joining fully in its achievement....

...Above all, it was now clear that the ECSC method was indeed the way to establish the greatest solidarity among peoples. I spelled out the lesson before the Common Assembly:

"We can never sufficiently emphasize that the six Community countries are the fore-runners of a broader united Europe, whose bounds are set only by those who have not yet joined. Our Community is not a coal and steel producers' association: it is the beginning of Europe."

The beginning of Europe was a political conception; but, even more, it was a moral idea. Europeans had gradually lost the ability to live together and combine their creative strength. There seemed to be decline in their contribution to progress and to the civilization which they themselves had created—doubtless because in a changing world they no longer had institutions capable of leading them ahead. National institutions had proved that they were ill-adapted to this task. The new Community institutions, it seemed to me, were the only vehicle through which Europeans could once more deploy the exceptional qualities they had displayed in times past; and I did my best to make my listeners in the Assembly share this view:

"A long time ago, I was struck by an observation made by the Swiss philosopher Henri-Frédéric Amiel: 'Each man's experience starts again from the beginning. Only institutions grow wiser: they accumulate collective experience; and, owing to this experience and this wisdom, men subject to the same rules will not see their own nature changing, but their behavior gradually transformed.' If justification were needed for our common institutions, that is it. When I think that Frenchmen, Germans, Belgians, Dutchmen, Italians, and Luxembourgers are obeying the same rules and, by doing so, are now seeing their common problems in the same light; when I reflect that this will fundamentally change their behavior one to another—then I tell myself that definitive progress is being made in relations among the countries and peoples of Europe."

22

JEAN MONNET

Seeds of the Pleven Plan

September 16, 1950

In this memorandum to Robert Schuman and Prime Minister René Pleven, Monnet expressed his fear that America's demand that Germany be rearmed risked the failure of the Schuman Plan negotiations. In an earlier letter to Pleven, dated September 3, 1950, and found in the Jean Monnet archives in Lausanne, Monnet had requested that the French government take the lead, because "what is needed is a universal political vision inspired by the same principle that informed the Schuman Plan: transform the existing state of affairs."

Jean Monnet–Robert Schuman Correspondance, 1947–1953 (Lausanne: Fondation Jean Monnet pour l'Europe, 1986), 58–59. Translated by Paul Hurwit.

1. Developments in Korea[1] have caused everyone to accept the fact that German participation was essential to the defense of the West. This is an obvious necessity. But it means that we have to confront a choice that we must make without delay. Either we will resign ourselves to historical fatality, and we will bring once again into the international community a Germany that has at its disposal armed forces and all of the attributes of sovereignty; or else, in accordance with the Schuman Plan, Germany will be integrated into continental Western Europe. In this way, we can hasten the establishment of this Western Europe that is indispensable to the Atlantic defense and to the prosperity of the community of free peoples. At the same time, the sense of belonging to the European community will replace the German nationalistic and military mentality.

In short, we need to know whether we are dealing with Germany or continental Europe. If the latter, we can provide a positive solution to the German Question. If, though, we are dealing with Germany in isolation, we will prevent the founding of Europe.

2. Setting up on a national basis the requisite German participation in the common defense, instead of integrating Germany into Western Europe, would enable that country to go its own way. A decision of this kind and the freedom of action which, from this perspective, would be restored to Germany as a recompense would give it the means and, depending on circumstances, the temptation to oscillate between West and East. In the final analysis, German rearmament within a national framework, far from strengthening Western Europe, would leave it more disunited, that is, weaker than it is today.

The result on the continent would be greater moral disarray than that which preceded the Schuman proposal. The neighboring countries would keep an anxious watch over the possible adventures of a rearmed Germany strengthened by its industrial and demographic potential and using it for its own nationalistic purposes as a result of its restored sovereignty.

3. The Schuman Plan could also fail in the event that the current negotiations do not prove successful or that they end with a purely technical agreement covering coal and steel, but that has no political significance or future.

The Schuman Plan must and can be both the beginning of the creation of a Western Europe structured at France's initiative and, at the

[1]The Korean War began on June 25, 1950, when North Korea invaded South Korea.

same time, the only possible resolution of the German Question, that is, by the political and material integration of Germany into a supranational community composed also of France, Italy, and the Benelux countries.

The pooling of coal and steel outputs, the creation of a single market, the inauguration of a supranational High Authority and a Common Assembly can put in place the first economic and psychological bulwarks of this community. Other achievements can then follow, gradually expanding the union of the nationhood of countries that until then had been disunited and adversarial.

4. If the Germans were to gain the immediate advantages they were hoping for under the Schuman Plan, but independently of the latter, that is, if they were to take part in the Western defense on a national basis, in which case their current status would be modified, we would run the risk of having them turn away from us and of seeing nationalistic fervor once more gain the ascendancy.

In this case, the implementation of the Schuman Plan and the building of Europe would become impossible.

5. German opinion is already showing reluctance and division. Some of the German representatives, such as Professor [Walter] Hallstein, who, as far as we can judge, mirror Chancellor Adenauer's convictions, remain supporters of the Schuman Plan and of the establishment of a Western Europe of which Germany would be a true integral part. Others among them, whose voices gain strength each day, are exhibiting purely national concerns.

6. For all of these reasons, in my view we should examine the two proposals that follow, with reference to Item 4 of the agenda published in the press release of the evening of the 15th.

1. That Germany's participation in the common defense should come under the supranational European purview of an expanded Schuman Plan, which was devised on France's initiative and to whose formulation Great Britain and the United States contributed.
2. That it be acknowledged:
   a. That the Atlantic Community includes:
      - The United States,
      - Great Britain and the British Commonwealth,
      - The countries in the western part of the Continent;
   b. That the defense and other agencies of this community must be linked together on that basis;

c. That, within this community, the Western nations must, in accordance with the principles set forth in the Schuman Plan on France's initiative, pursue the effort that they have undertaken in order to create a continental community.

This interlocking arrangement would, with the necessary modifications, impart to the existing entities of the Atlantic Community an effectiveness that they now lack.

23

RENÉ PLEVEN

Pleven Plan for a European Defense Community (EDC)

October 24, 1950

In a statement to the National Assembly, excerpted here, the French prime minister announced the Pleven Plan, a supranational defense community modeled on the Schuman Plan. Contingent on the successful completion of Schuman Plan negotiations, it envisaged the creation of a European defense ministry responsible to an assembly and a council of defense ministers. The National Assembly accepted the proposal in principle as a further step toward the integration of West Germany into Western Europe. The Schuman Plan talks ended on April 18, 1951, when six nations signed and later ratified the Treaty of Paris, creating the European Coal and Steel Community (ECSC). The treaty establishing the European Defense Community (EDC) was signed on May 27, 1952, by the six ECSC nations but was ratified by only four. Italy and France failed to approve the treaty.

Pleven Plan available at http://www.ena.lu/mce.cfm; also available in English at http://www.iue.it/; also in *Documents on European Union*, ed. and trans. A. G. Harryvan and J. van der Harst (New York: St. Martin's Press, 1997), 65–69. ECSC and other EU treaties available at http://europa.eu/abc/treaties/index_en.htm and http://www.iue.it/; also in *Treaties Establishing the European Communities (ECSC, EEC, EAEC), Single European Act, Other Basic Instruments*, abridged edition (Luxembourg: Office for Official Publications of the European Communities, 1987).

Germany, albeit not a party to the Atlantic Pact,[1] will nevertheless also benefit from the resulting security system. It is, therefore, only right for Germany to make its contribution to the defense of Western Europe. That is why the Government has decided to take the initiative and make the following declaration, in order to open up the discussion of this important issue in the National Assembly.

The solution to the problem of the German contribution must be uncompromising and sought without delay, looking both at the potential for immediate action and towards a future united Europe. . . .

Merely responding to events, however, is unlikely to provide a constructive solution. Any system that led, whether immediately or eventually, directly or not, with or without conditions, to the creation of a German army would give rise to renewed distrust and suspicion. The formation of German divisions, of a German Ministry of Defense, would sooner or later be bound to lead to the rebuilding of a national army and, by that token, to the revival of German militarism. This kind of outcome, which our allies have at all events unanimously condemned, would be a danger to Germany itself.

We hope that the signing of the coal and steel plan will very soon seal the agreement of the six participating countries, which will give all the peoples of Europe a guarantee that Western European coal and steel industries cannot be used for aggressive purposes.

As soon as the Plan has been signed, the French Government wants to see a solution to the question of Germany's contribution to the creation of a European force that takes heed of the cruel lessons of the past and looks forward to the kind of future that so many Europeans from all countries hope to see in Europe.

It proposes the creation, for the purposes of common defense, of a European army tied to the political institutions of a united Europe.

This proposal is directly inspired by the recommendation adopted by the Assembly of the Council of Europe on 11 August 1950, calling for the immediate creation of a unified European army with a view to cooperating with American and Canadian forces in the defense of peace.

A European army cannot be created simply by placing national military units side by side, since, in practice, this would merely mask a coalition of the old sort. Tasks that can be tackled only in common must be matched by common institutions. A united European army,

[1]The North Atlantic Treaty, signed on April 4, 1949, by twelve nations, was a defensive alliance viewed by the United States as part of its strategy of containing communism.

made up of forces from the various European nations must, as far as possible, pool all of its human and material components under a single political and military European authority.

The Member Governments would appoint a Minister for Defense who would be accountable, in a manner yet to be determined, to those appointing him and to a European Assembly. This assembly could be the Strasbourg Assembly, or an offshoot of it, or an assembly made up of specially elected delegates. He would have the same powers over the European army that a national Minister for Defense has over his country's national forces. He would be responsible in particular for implementing such general directives as he might receive from a Council made up of Ministers from the participant countries. He would serve as the official channel between the European Community and third countries or international bodies as regards all aspects involved in the performance of his task.

The contingents provided by the participating countries would be incorporated in the European army, at the level of the smallest possible unit.

The European army would be financed from a common budget. The European Minister for Defense would be tasked with implementing existing international undertakings and negotiating and implementing new international undertakings on the basis of directives from the Council of Ministers. The European armaments and equipment program would be adopted and conducted under his authority.

Participant states that already have national forces would retain their authority over those of their existing forces that were not incorporated into the European army.

Conversely, the European Minister for Defense could, with the authorization of the Council of Ministers, place back at the disposal of a member government a part of its national forces forming part of the European force in order to meet requirements other than those of common defense.

The European forces placed at the disposal of the unified Atlantic command would respect the obligations entered into under the Atlantic Pact, as regards both general strategy and organization and equipment. . . .

It is on this basis that the French Government proposes to invite Great Britain and the free countries of continental Europe that agree to take part in creating the European army jointly to devise how the principles that we have set out can be put into practice. This work is to begin in Paris as soon as the coal and steel plan is signed.

24

DWIGHT EISENHOWER

A Call for Political Unity and the Economic Integration of Western Europe

July 3, 1951

At a dinner in his honor at the English-Speaking Union in London, where he had gone to honor the Americans killed in World War II, General Dwight Eisenhower, NATO's supreme allied commander in Europe, urged the European peoples to unite to secure their future against the Communist threat. Once unity was achieved, he argued, Europe could build adequate security and continue "the march of human betterment that has characterized western civilization." Winston Churchill, British prime minister Clement Attlee, and nearly a thousand dinner guests heard his much-praised speech, reprinted in part here. Eisenhower's enthusiasm for European unity foreshadowed his own conversion to supporting the EDC.

In the scale of values of the English-speaking people, freedom is the first and most precious right. Without it, no other right can be exercised, and human existence loses all significance. This unity of ours in fundamentals is an international fact. . . .

. . . In any case, may we never forget that our common devotion to deep human values and our mutual trust are the bedrock of our joint strength.

In that spirit our countries are joined with the peoples of Western Europe and the North Atlantic to defend the freedoms of western civilization. Opposed to us—cold and forbidding—is an ideological front that marshals every weapon in the arsenal of dictatorship. Subversion, propaganda, deceit and the threat of naked force are daily hurled against us and our friends in a globe-encircling, relentless campaign. . . .

The stand in Korea should serve notice in this area, as well as in the Far East, that we will resist naked aggression with all the force at

---

Dwight Eisenhower, *Vital Speeches of the Day*, 17, no. 20 (August 1, 1951): 613–14.

our command. Our effort to provide security against the possibility of another and even greater emergency which will never be of our making—must go forward with the same resolution and courage that has characterized our Korean forces. The member nations in the North Atlantic Treaty Organization need not fear the future or any Communistic threat—if we are alert, realistic and resolute. Our community possesses a potential might that far surpasses the sinister forces of slave camp and chained millions. But to achieve the serenity and confidence that our potential can provide, we must press forward with the mobilization of our spiritual and intellectual strength; we must develop promptly the material force that will assure the safety of our friends upon the continent and the security of the free world.

This is the challenge of our times that, until satisfactorily met, establishes priorities in all our thoughts, our work, our sacrifices. The hand of the aggressor is stayed by strength—and strength alone.

Although the security of each of us is bound up in the safety of all of us, the immediate threat is most keenly felt by our partners in Europe. Half the continent is already within the monolithic mass of totalitarianism. The drawn and haunted faces in the docks of the purge courts are grim evidence of what Communistic domination means. It is clearly necessary that we quickly develop maximum strength within free Europe itself. Our own interests demand it.

It is a truism that where, among partners, strength is demanded in its fullness, unity is the first requisite. Without unity, the effort becomes less powerful in application, less decisive in result. This fact has special application in Europe. It would be difficult indeed to overstate the benefits, in these years of stress and tension, that would accrue to NATO if the free nations of Europe were truly a unit. . . .

European leaders, seeking a sound and wise solution, are spurred by the vision of a man at this table—a man of inspiring courage in dark hours, of wise counsel in grave decisions. Winston Churchill's plea for a united Europe can yet bear such greatness of fruit that it may well be remembered as the most notable achievement of a career marked by achievement.

The difficulties of integrating Western Europe, of course, appear staggering to those who live by ritual. But great majorities in Europe earnestly want liberty, peace, and the opportunity to pass on to their children the fair lands and the culture of Western Europe. They deserve, at the very least, a fair chance to work together for the common purpose; freed of the costly encumbrances they are now compelled to carry.

Europe cannot attain the towering material stature possible to its people's skills and spirit so long as it is divided by patchwork territorial fences. They foster localized instead of common interest. They pyramid every cost with middlemen, tariffs, taxes, and overheads. Barred, absolutely, are the efficient division of labor and resources and the easy flow of trade. In the political field, these barriers promote distrust and suspicion. They serve vested interests at the expense of peoples and prevent truly concerted action for Europe's own and obvious good. . . .

But with unity achieved, Europe could build adequate security and, at the same time, continue the march of human betterment that has characterized western civilization. Once united, the farms and factories of France and Belgium, the foundries of Germany, the rich farmlands of Holland and Denmark, the skilled labor of Italy, will produce miracles for the common good. In such unity is a secure future for these peoples. It would mean early independence of aid from America and other Atlantic countries. The coffers, mines and factories of that continent are not inexhaustible. Dependence upon them must be minimized by the maximum in cooperative effort. The establishment of a workable European federation would go far to create confidence among people everywhere that Europe was doing its full and vital share in giving this cooperation.

25

JOHAN WILLEM BEYEN

Beyen Plan to Establish a Customs Union

December 11, 1952

Foreign minister of the Netherlands Johan Willem Beyen, an ardent opponent of the sectoral approach to integration, stressed the need to integrate whole economies. In this memo, excerpted here, he proposed a customs union. Beyen's proposals were central to the negotiations leading to the Treaties of Rome in 1957.

"Beyen Plan," in *Documents on European Union*, ed. and trans. A. G. Harryvan and J. van der Harst (New York: St. Martin's Press, 1997), 71–74.

In the opinion of the Netherlands Government, economic integration as well as the monetary and social coordination it implies, is therefore of essential importance to the extension of the interests of European countries as it is a prerequisite to maintaining and improving the standard of living, including all social aspects, and may serve to reinforce the defense efforts. It will not be possible to maintain and gradually improve the standard of living in Europe—in spite of the steady increase of the population—without raising and improving European production and increasing productivity, which cannot be achieved in a Europe divided into a number of limited markets as a result of trade barriers and subject to monetary instability. . . .

2. Within a certain number of years a Tariffs Community should be established, which would result in the complete abolition of import duties within the Community and would introduce a new general tariff of import duties *vis-à-vis* non-participating States. . . .
   a. It will be necessary to level the existing tariff walls hampering the stabilization and the expansion of markets and consequently restricting production, which in their turn stand in the way of a rising standard of living in Europe. . . .
   c. Under the system envisaged by the Netherlands Government it will be incumbent not on the national Governments, but on the Community to give effect to these clauses. . . .

26

JOHN FOSTER DULLES

Alarmed by French Rejection of the European Defense Community Treaty

August 31, 1954

In this excerpt from a statement issued to the press, U.S. secretary of state John Foster Dulles expressed his grave disappointment at the failure of the French National Assembly on August 30, 1954, to ratify the EDC treaty.

Foreign Relations of the United States, 1952–1954, V, 1120–22.

The French rejection of the European Defense Community is a saddening event. France thus turns away from her own historic proposal made nearly four years ago. That proposal sought a unification of the military strength of Continental Europe into a single European army so as to end the era of recurrent European wars, the last two of which became world wars.

The French action does not change certain basic and stubborn facts:

a. The effective defense of Continental Europe calls for a substantial military contribution from the Germans; yet all, including the Germans themselves, would avoid national re-armament in a form which could be misused by resurgent militarism.

b. Germany cannot be subjected indefinitely to neutrality or otherwise be discriminated against in terms of her sovereignty including the inherent right of individual and collective self-defense. Limitations on German sovereignty to be permanently acceptable must be shared by others as part of a collective international order.

c. The prevention of war between neighboring nations which have a long record of fighting cannot be dependably achieved merely by national promises or threats, but only by merging certain functions of government into supranational institutions.

To deal with these facts was the lofty purpose of EDC. Four of the six prospective members of EDC had ratified that treaty—Belgium, Germany, Luxembourg and the Netherlands. A fifth, Italy, was on the point of ratifying it. The U.K. and the U.S. had made far-reaching commitments of association with EDC. France thus disassociates herself not only from her own proposal but from her prospective partners who had stood united at the recent Brussels Conference.

The U.S. post-war policies beginning in 1946 were framed on the assumption that Western Europe would at long last develop a unity which would make it immune from war as between its members and defensible against aggression from without. The imperative need for that unity was recognized by the leading statesmen of all the free nations of Europe. The U.S. joined the North Atlantic Treaty defensive alliance with the Western European countries. We assisted these countries to recover from the weakening of World War II. Both on the economic and military side we made massive contributions. We stationed the equivalent of 6 divisions in Europe. We furthermore made our leading military figures available to assume high positions in the military organization designed to defend Western Europe.

The French negative action, without the provision of any alternative, obviously imposes on the United States the obligation to reappraise its foreign policies, particularly those in relation to Europe. The need for such a review can scarcely be questioned since the North Atlantic Council of Ministers has itself twice declared with unanimity that the EDC was of paramount importance to the European defense it planned. Furthermore, such review is required by conditions which the Congress attached this year and last year to authorizations and appropriations for military contributions to Europe.

The Western nations now owe it to the Federal Republic of Germany to do quickly all that lies in their power to restore sovereignty to that Republic and to enable it to contribute to international peace and security. The existing Treaty to restore sovereignty is by its terms contingent upon the coming into force of EDC. It would be unconscionable if the failure to realize EDC through no fault of Germany's should now be used as an excuse for penalizing Germany. The Federal German Republic should take its place as a free and equal member of the society of nations. That was the purport of the resolution which the United States Senate adopted unanimously last July, and the United States will act accordingly.

The United States stands ready to support the many in Western Europe who despite their valiant efforts are left in grave anxiety. We need not feel that the European idea is dead merely because, in one of the six countries, a present majority seems against one of its manifestations. There is still much on which to build and those foundations should not be shaken by any abrupt or any ill-considered action of our own.

It is a tragedy that in one country nationalism, abetted by Communism, has asserted itself so as to endanger the whole of Europe. That tragedy would be compounded if the United States was thereby led to conclude that it must turn to a course of narrow nationalism. It is a matter of elementary prudence that the United States should review its dispositions and planning in the light of the new situation now created. We are fortunately so situated that we do not need to identify ourselves with what to us seem self-defeating policies. We have flexibility to adjust our own policies to take account of developments elsewhere. In doing so, we shall be governed by the realization that we cannot in isolation find safety for ourselves.

3

The Road to Closer Union and the Treaties of Rome

27

The Messina Declaration

June 1–2, 1955

The foreign ministers of the six ECSC countries met in Messina, Italy, to discuss further European integration after the EDC debacle. They appointed René Mayer to succeed Monnet as president of the ECSC's High Authority and Spaak to chair an intergovernmental committee to consider various proposals for a common market. In his 1971 book, The Continuing Battle: Memoirs of a European, *Spaak described the communiqué they adopted, excerpted here, as "bold" and wrote that the foreign ministers realized "the political importance of their goal," which "was nothing short of a revolution." He expressed the hope that one day Britain might join the six countries in their efforts to unite Europe.*

The governments of the Federal Republic of Germany, Belgium, France, Italy, Luxembourg, and the Netherlands believe the time has come to take a new step on the road of European construction. They are of the opinion that this objective should be achieved first of all in the economic sphere.

They believe that the establishment of a united Europe must be

Messina Declaration, available at http://www.eu-history.leidenuniv.nl/index.php3?c=52#; also in *Documents on European Union*, ed. and trans. A. G. Harryvan and J. van der Harst (New York: St. Martin's Press, 1997), 92–94.

achieved through the development of common institutions, the progressive fusion of national economies, the creation of a common market, and the gradual harmonization of their social policies.

Such an agenda seems indispensable to them if Europe is to preserve the standing which she has in the world, to restore the influence and her prestige, and to improve steadily the living standard of the population.

To these ends, the six ministers have agreed on the following objectives:

1. The growth of trade and the migration of the population require the joint development of the main channels of communication. To this end, a joint study will be undertaken of development plans oriented to establishing a European network of canals, motorways, electric rail lines, and for a standardization of equipment, as well as research for a better coordination of air transport.

2. Putting more abundant energy at a cheaper price at the disposal of the European economies constitutes a fundamental element of economic progress. That is why all arrangements should be made to develop sufficient exchanges of gas and electric power capable of increasing the profitability of investments and reducing the supply costs. Studies will be undertaken of methods to coordinate development prospects for the production and consumption of energy, and to draw up general guidelines for an overall policy.

3. The development of atomic energy for peaceful purposes will very soon open up the prospect of a new industrial revolution beyond comparison with that of the last hundred years. The signatory states believe they must study the creation of a joint organization to which will be assigned the responsibility and the means to secure the peaceful development of atomic energy while taking into consideration the special commitments of certain governments with third parties.

These means should include:

a. the establishment of a common fund supported by the contribution of each of the participating countries, and allowing for the financing of power plants and for current or future energy research;

b. free and adequate access to raw materials, the free exchange of information, by-products and special equipment, and the mobility of technicians;

c. making available any benefits and financial subsidies without discrimination, towards the development of energy sources;

d. cooperation with non-member states.

The Objective of the "Common Market"

The six governments acknowledge that the constitution of a European Common Market free of internal duties and all quantitative restrictions is the goal of their action in the realm of economic policy. They believe that this market should be achieved in stages. The realization of this objective requires study of the following questions:

a. The procedure and the pace of the gradual suppression of obstacles to trade in relations between the participating countries, as well as appropriate steps leading to the gradual standardization of tariffs applying to non-member states;

b. The measures to be taken for harmonizing the general policy of the participating states in the financial, economic, and social fields;

c. The adoption of practical steps to ensure an adequate coordination of the monetary policies of the member states, in order to allow for the creation and developments of a common market;

d. A system of escape clauses;

e. The creation and operation of a currency re-adoption fund;

f. The gradual introduction of free circulation of labor;

g. The development of rules assuring the free play of competition within the common market, particularly in such a way as to exclude all preferences of a national basis;

h. The institutional agencies appropriate for the realization and operating of the common market.

The creation of a European Investment Fund will be studied. This Fund should have as its object the joint development of European economic projects, and especially the development of the less favored regions of the participating states.

As for the social field, the six governments believe it is essential to study the progressive harmonization of regulations now in force in the different states, particularly those relating to the length of the work-day and the payment of additional benefits (overtime work, Sunday and holiday work, the length of vacations, and vacation allowances).

28

JEAN MONNET

A United Europe Would Stabilize East-West Relations

June 16, 1955

In an interview by the writer André Fontaine for the French newspaper Le Monde, *excerpted here, Monnet argued that a united Europe would produce a dynamism that would enable Europeans to "hold their own" between the cold war superpowers. Monnet expressed his strong support for German reunification, countering many critics of the European movement, especially in Germany, who saw European unity as part of a French plan to prevent it.*

[Fontaine:] *Mr. President, at this moment when you are stepping down from your functions at the High Authority of the European Coal and Steel Community, the six foreign affairs ministers meeting in Messina have just adopted a program for European revival. What is your feeling about the prospects that this decision has opened up?*

[Monnet:] The Messina Conference has revived the idea of Europe. There was agreement about the objectives. But, as to the means, the

Jean Monnet Archives, Fondation Jean Monnet pour l'Europe, Lausanne. Translated by Paul Hurwit.

ministers agreed to meet again on October 1 to decide on the path we will all travel under their leadership. This is a decisive moment. We must learn whether we're heading for the United States of Europe or whether we're falling back to a Society of Nations.

As to the choice the governments involved will make for us, what is important is less the step we must take than the direction in which they are pushing us. If they restrict themselves to purely nationalist formulas that have so tragically failed in the past, since they could not prevent war, we will hear the governments talk about cooperation. But if, on the other hand, these governments decide to make things new, then we will know that they have consented to transfer to a common authority the powers which they can no longer exercise separately for the benefit of each of our countries. It is only by instituting this change that we can secure our safety.

Do you continue to believe, then, that no other way to build Europe exists apart from the transfer of power to a supranational authority?

The word "supranational" is often poorly understood. You could interpret it to mean that nations submit to an external, foreign power, while, in truth, it means instituting federal ties among the European nations.

Of course, various technical elements are possible, but we shouldn't stop at simple cooperation among governments. If decisions have to be arrived at unanimously, then it's the veto and, therefore, immobility. If decisions require a majority, there's the risk of a coalition of governments acting to the detriment of one of the partners. The only way out of this alternative is the delegation of some part of the powers of the States to a common authority, that is, to a federal institution whose members are the representatives of all of the participating countries....

Has this conviction been confirmed by your own experience after two and one-half years at the head of the High Authority of the European Coal and Steel Community? Can you cite the basic lessons you learned from this experience?

The Coal and Steel Community shows us that the building of a great European market of 160 million consumers, which is essential to a rise in the standard of living, is not only possible, but easier than we thought.

It showed us, too, that this common market cannot operate unless it adheres to rules that are the same for everyone and that apply at the same time to States, companies, and to consumers.

It showed us, furthermore, that transitional measures are needed so that we can move smoothly from isolated markets to their merger into a common market, but that this rearrangement can happen all the more rapidly because all of those concerned know that the transitional measures have a purpose.

By solving the concrete problems of the coal and steel market, we have at the same time been led to solutions that apply to general problems that affect the economy in its entirety, such as the problems of taxes and freight rates.

These rules could be administered, these transitions worked out, these solutions delineated only because there is a common authority that makes decisions for the good of everyone. . . .

But some protest this way of transferring sovereignty by maintaining that it will in the end limit the scope of a rebuilt Europe by leaving some countries aside.

There was never a question of limiting Europe to any given number of countries. The Schuman Plan was proposed to Germany and to all countries wishing to participate in it. It so happened that, insofar as coal and steel are concerned, six countries agreed to the plan. The number of countries that, according to the Messina projections, were to take part in the plan as it unfolded was not set in advance. I trust that others will join the six countries of the Coal and Steel Community. As we move forward toward the United States of Europe, I have no doubt that, when they see the results we will have achieved, other countries will become members of the plan or join together in this venture, and will, therefore, expand the scope of European unification.

Look at what happened with Great Britain. A major step was taken on December 21 of last year with the partnership agreement between the Community and the United Kingdom, which was signed both by the High Authority and by the governments. During the ratification debate in the House of Commons, both the government and the Opposition stated that this agreement marked the beginning of a growing relationship and that it could be the model for Great Britain and the Continental countries of new measures that they can take together. This is one more reason to keep going in this same direction.

Yet Europe has risen from the ruins, and production is now ongoing in all of the countries. Isn't it at all understandable that public opinion might feel less inclined to support European unification and that we are even seeing another surge of nationalist, if not nationalistic, feelings in Western Europe?

It happens quite often today that the European nations are not conscious of the changes that are occurring on the outside, or of the choices being made on their behalf. However, the current prosperity should not hide the fact that the European countries are finding themselves more and more in a weakened position. The United States and the Soviet Union are growing at a faster pace than we are. Right now, the countries of Western Europe are allies that receive protection and aid and are caught in the dispute between the United States and the Soviet Union. If the Americans and Russians are making faster progress, it's not because they have a capacity for inventiveness, work, and organization that is greater than the Europeans' own. The Europeans have a capacity that is at least the equal of the others. It's because the United States and the Soviet Union, even while their regimes are different, show growth on a continental scale. In our case, though, the undertakings, the resources, and the markets are still walled off from each other.

In order for the Europeans to help keep the peace and improve their standard of living under the conditions that prevail today, we must unite what is divided while there is still time. This is why it's so important that the objectives the ministers set at Messina become reality. . . .

Will this unification of Europe and this creation of common institutions cause the disappearance of nations, or can you tell us, to the contrary, that in your view the national idea must still remain in the United States of Europe?

The gradual institution of a European market as huge as the American one means expansion and modernization of production, a rising standard of living, and an improved destiny for workers. How could that harm the individual personality of each nation?

The common institutions we need are federal entities, not those of a unitary State. The powers that have to be transferred to them are limited to those that nationalist States can no longer exercise for the benefit of the countries concerned. As integration proceeds, it will promote the flowering of this diversity, which forms a preponderant part of Europe's richness.

Doesn't German dynamism seem to you to pose a threat to the European federation, given that it might dominate the community?

Even supposing that such a threat exists, which I do not believe, since I have confidence in my compatriots, it would most definitely be greater if our countries remained separated by rivalries. Federal rules and institutions remove the factors tending toward domination that are inseparable from national sovereignty and nationalism. With these rules and institutions brought together in a great market, there would be no dynamism of just one country, but rather expansion of all of the participating nations.

We have in Western Europe one long-standing example of a federal community. This is Switzerland. Switzerland is made up of constituent populations that speak German, French, and Italian. The German-speaking Swiss are the largest part of the population and hold the largest share of Swiss industrial potential. But because Switzerland is organized into a federation, the German-speaking people do not dominate.

Everyone knows that Europe can be built only if the old Franco-German antagonism is removed. Consequently, for the sake of all of the countries that want to be part of a united Europe, France and Germany must unambiguously take this path. For the benefit of France, Germany, and Europe, the French and German peoples must leave no doubt as to the choice that they want to make and which they will unwaveringly adhere to, along with the other countries that are already members of the Coal and Steel Community and with all those that will accept the authority of European federal institutions and regulations. . . .

The current détente is changing international prospects fairly substantially. Do you think that the creation of a European federation can help to strengthen it further?

Peaceful intentions, treaties, are not enough to guarantee peace. German unity or an agreement on armaments does not lay the foundations for coexistence. As long as the European peoples remain divided, their weaknesses and their separate policies will make an issue out of each one and a permanent cause of distrust and instability between East and West. The relations between East and West can become normal and stabilized only if, by bringing about their union in a United States of Europe, the European countries come to possess a dynamism that lets them hold their own in the face of the energy of the United States and the Soviet Union.

It is absolutely essential the West and East Germans reunite. By reunifying them within the framework of European unification, it will be possible to achieve at the same time German unity and coexistence, that is, a lasting peace.

No one believes that your departure from Luxembourg marks the end of your service to Europe. Can you give us an idea of how you will continue that service?

One must have recourse to the public opinion of the European countries to achieve concrete objectives. Each person must look to see what the United States of Europe means to him and to the improvement of his working and daily lives.

In my view, public opinion in the countries of Europe is more enterprising than the governments often are. This public opinion is aware that the governments come up each day against problems of all kinds that cannot be solved using the methods of the past, and that a change is essential. This change will be the gradual creation of the United States of Europe, which is the pressing need and great hope of our time.

The practical implementation of the Messina resolution is our next step.

In order to persuade the governments to make the choice that they have put off and to propose to their Parliament the federal institutions required, the political parties, the unions, and all supporters of European unity must, of necessity and with haste, organize themselves so that they can make their conviction known to the public and the governments.

As for me, I will, of course, do everything I can to ensure that these outcomes are achieved without delay.

29

JEAN MONNET

Action Committee for the United States of Europe

October 6, 1955

The international Action Committee for the United States of Europe was created and run by Monnet and its multilingual secretary-general, Dutch foreign ministry official Max Kohnstamm. It was composed of political party and trade union leaders, civil servants, and current government officials and became an effective lobby for integration in all six countries. The memorandum by Monnet, excerpted here, explained its goals.

Experience has shown that, despite the European peoples' aspiration for unity, the building of the United States of Europe has, to date, lacked a suitable popular and political base.

"The Action Committee for the United States of Europe," whose formation is being announced today, must establish new circumstances, in which the political parties and workers' unions will be the impetus driving the building of Europe. . . .

By virtue of their adherence to the rules of democracy, the Committee and the member organizations will work by consultation with governments, legislatures, and public opinion. Their initiatives will be political in nature. The Committee will be financially autonomous, and its expenses will be covered by contributions from the member organizations.

The Committee founders believe that the European Movement and the agencies serving it must continue their propaganda campaign in favor of the idea of [a united] Europe. . . .

Armed with this program of action, the Committee founders will now ask their respective organizations (political parties or unions) to join the Committee and to appoint delegates.

The formation of the Committee and the merging of political and union forces toward European union come at an opportune moment.

Jean Monnet Archives, Fondation Jean Monnet pour l'Europe, Lausanne AMK 2/5/11. Translated by Paul Hurwit.

The "Action Committee for the United States of Europe" and its member organizations must strive to encourage the interested governments to pursue energetically "the revival of Europe" and to bring about true progress toward European federation through the work begun in Brussels by the Commission, chaired by Mr. Paul-Henri Spaak, which is charged with implementation of the Messina resolution. The eminent status of the founders of the Action Committee for the United States of Europe represents, with respect to public opinion, the guarantee of a will to change.

30

JEAN MONNET

"The Spearhead" for European Unity Must Be "the Peaceful Atom"

January 1956

Monnet's Action Committee, at his initiative, passed a resolution asserting the urgent need to establish a European atomic energy community (Euratom), which he viewed as the path to European union. In his Memoirs, *he quoted passages from this resolution and then commented on its importance.*

The text on which I now knew our Committee would unanimously agree called on the Governments to set up Euratom without delay:

> Action is urgently needed if Europe is not to let her opportunity pass by.
>
> An atomic industry producing atomic energy will inevitably be able to produce bombs. For that reason the political aspects and the economic aspects of atomic energy are inseparable. The European Community must develop atomic energy exclusively for peaceful purposes. This choice requires a watertight system of control. It opens the way to general control on a world-wide scale. . . .

Jean Monnet, *Memoirs* (Garden City, N.Y.: Doubleday, 1978), 418–19.

> In order that the necessary measures may be taken rapidly, we have agreed to submit the attached declaration for Parliamentary approval in Belgium, France, Germany, Italy, Luxembourg, and the Netherlands, and to invite our Governments to conclude without delay a Treaty conforming to the rules set forth therein.

The declaration that followed called for the establishment of a Community on the model of the ECSC. The Commission which was to be its executive body was to be the sole owner of nuclear fuels, whether imported or home-produced, and to monitor their use from beginning to end. The Commission was to have the sole right to negotiate and conclude agreements with non-member countries; it was also to be responsible for the security rules. This plan was in accordance with the work being done by the experts in Brussels. . . .

. . . All agreed with the Action Committee's aim:

> The development of atomic energy for peaceful uses opens the prospect of a new industrial revolution and the possibility of a profound change in living and working conditions.
>
> Together, our countries are capable of themselves developing a nuclear industry. They form the only region in the world that can attain the same level as the great world Powers. Yet separately they will not be able to overcome their time-lag which is a consequence of European disunity.

If the Euratom project was unanimously agreed on by the Committee, this was because it benefited from the convergence of two complementary lines of thought. The French saw it as guaranteeing greater independence in energy, through a joint effort; for the Germans, it was a way to enter the atomic age, but for peaceful purposes only. For Ollenhauer's[1] friends, this proviso was the express condition of any agreement and very largely the justification of their presence on the Committee. I agreed with them that it was essential for the ownership and control of fissile materials to be vested in Euratom. For the majority of French people, an atomic energy Community was a clear and distinct ideal—while that of an economic Community remained nebulous. For some Germans, on the other hand, the Common Market was the only dynamic element in the relaunching of Europe, but one for which they would have to pay the price of Euratom and its dirigiste approach. So we had no choice: the spearhead for the unification of Europe would have to be the peaceful atom.

[1]Erich Ollenhauer, leader of the German Social Democratic party (SPD).

31

KONRAD ADENAUER

Unreserved German Support for European Integration

January 19, 1956

In this forceful directive to his cabinet ministers, West German chancellor Konrad Adenauer demanded they have a "clear, positive attitude" toward European integration. He believed it was necessary for Germany's future in Europe and its relations with France and key to Western Europe's relations with the Soviet Union and the United States. Adenauer's biographer Hans-Peter Schwarz wrote that the chancellor, in concluding remarks not excerpted here, stressed several points: the importance of establishing a common market with the Six and creating "joint institutions" to facilitate the functioning of the common market and "promote further political development"; integration in the transportation sector; and "the foundation of a European nuclear energy community."

The current international situation bears extraordinary dangers. Determined measures are required to avert them and to induce a positive course of events. Above all this includes a clear, positive German attitude to European integration.

The key statesmen of the West consider developments to hinge on this European integration, as evidenced in particular in my talks with [Antoine] Pinay and [Paul-Henri] Spaak and very specific American political declarations. This view is undoubtedly correct. If integration is successful, we can add the weight of a united Europe as an important new element into the balance of the negotiations on security as well as reunification. Conversely, one cannot expect serious concessions by the Soviet Union as long as Europe's division gives her hope to draw this or that country on her side, thereby breaking the cohe-

---

Konrad Adenauer, *Erinnerungen, 1955–1959* (Stuttgart: Deutsche Verlags-Anstalt, 1967), 253–55. Translated by Christian Ostermann. See also Hans-Peter Schwarz, *Konrad Adenauer: German Politician and Statesman in a Period of War, Revolution, and Reconstruction* (Providence, R.I.: Berghahn Books, 1997), 2:230–31.

sion of the West and inaugurating the step-by-step incorporation of Europe into the satellite system. In addition, a lasting arrangement of our relationship with France is only possible through European integration. Should integration fail due to our resistance or our hesitation, the consequences would be unpredictable.

From this follows as a guideline of our policy that we have to implement the Messina decision in a determined and genuine fashion. Even more strongly than before do we have to be mindful of the political nature of this decision, which is to create not only technical cooperation for technical considerations, but a community which—in the interest of reunification as well—assures the common direction of political will and action. The OEEC framework is insufficient for this purpose. All technical considerations have to serve this political objective. . . .

32

JOHN FOSTER DULLES

Strong U.S. Support for Euratom and Common Market Proposals

January 26, 1956

In a telegram to the U.S. embassies in the six European capitals on the eve of a visit to Washington by British prime minister Anthony Eden, Dulles outlined U.S. policy concerns regarding Europe and support for integration. Part of that telegram is reprinted here.

1. We welcome strong support UK has been giving to closer international cooperation among countries of Europe and Atlantic Community in NATO and OEEC framework. We do same.
2. But merely cooperative arrangements are not enough to meet three most serious problems in Europe:

Foreign Relations of the United States, 1955–1957, IV, 399–400.

a. Problem of tying Germany organically into Western Community so as to diminish danger that over time a resurgent German nationalism might trade neutrality for reunification with view seizing controlling position between East and West.
b. The weakness of France and need to provide positive alternative to neutralism and "defeatism" in that country.
c. The solidifying of new relationship between France and Germany which has been developing since 1950 through integration movement.

3. Therefore we are concerned about British coolness to six-country integration. We believe this movement is important because it is best hope for solving three foregoing problems. Its success would justify some sacrifice of traditional U.S. and U.K. interests to achieve it.

4. Six-country supranational Euratom would be a powerful means of binding Germany to West and may be most feasible means for achieving effective control over weapons-quality material. If genuinely supranational, Euratom program would be compatible with national cooperation in OEEC.

5. United States does not attach to common market proposals same immediate security and political significance as we do to Euratom. However we believe that a common market which results in a general reduction of international trade barriers could contribute constructively to European integration. We therefore look forward with interest to concrete six-country proposals and would welcome staff talks this subject.

33

ROBERT MARJOLIN

French Officialdom: Main Obstacle in Rome Treaty Negotiations

1956–March 1957

In this excerpt from his memoirs, Robert Marjolin, French foreign minister Christian Pineau's special adviser in the Brussels negotiations, analyzed the negotiations' success over strong French opposition. Because "peace reigned in Western Europe" under America's protection, he wrote, new initiatives were possible.

The treaty establishing a European Defense Community (EDC) was rejected by the French National Assembly on August 30, 1954. For a while, the proponents of a united Europe felt that their whole world had collapsed around them, that Europeanism was finished for good, that the old national antagonisms would return as fierce as ever, that the fragmentation of the Continent would be perpetuated in all areas—political, military and economic. In France, moreover, the bitter disputes over the EDC had left deep wounds that looked as if they might never heal; national unity, restored at the time of the Liberation under the aegis of General de Gaulle, seemed shattered. . . .

Yet less than three years later, the treaties establishing the Common Market and Euratom were ratified by the Parliaments of the Six, including the French Parliament, without any major difficulty. They were accepted, especially the treaty setting up the European Economic Community, by the greater part of public opinion, if not with enthusiasm, at least with the feeling that this was something inevitable and possibly beneficial. In retrospect, this is all the more surprising in that the Common Market's creation was a step towards a much closer unity of Europe than anything that had gone before. It was more significant in this respect than the Marshall Plan, which had been above all an operation of collective rescue, and than the ECSC, which only

---

Robert Marjolin, *Architect of European Unity: Memoirs, 1911–1986* (London: Weidenfeld and Nicolson, 1989), 276–307.

concerned two industries. More significant, too, than the projected EDC, whose realization was at best very uncertain and from which Gaullist France would certainly have withdrawn.

In the circles pledged to the construction of Europe the mood was now turning to elation; the feeling that many things, if not everything, had become possible was replacing the sense of frustration caused by the failure of the EDC. . . .

What was the origin, or rather what were the origins, of this event which, at least on the face of it, was a near-miracle? A few men had, it is true, worked zealously and perseveringly for it to come about, but their efforts would probably have remained unavailing or would not have succeeded completely if the economic and political climate in Europe (including France) and in the world as a whole had not changed imperceptibly over the previous two or three years, to the point where this slow process of change had produced, in relation to the prewar and immediate postwar periods, a radical transformation.

The essential fact was that peace reigned in Western Europe. People knew instinctively that the nations situated in this part of the world would never war against one another again. Depending on how one looked at human nature, this state of affairs could be seen either as the triumph of wisdom over blind violence, or as evidence of utter exhaustion. Either way, the fact remains that none of the great nations that had made European history—notably, France, Britain and Germany—any longer had territorial claims on the others. Much more important, the conditions of warfare had changed so much with the advent of the atomic weapon that each of these erstwhile great powers suddenly found itself, militarily, almost completely powerless.

As to the ever present threat from the East, it did not constitute a real danger as long as the United States remained in a position of world supremacy. . . . As of the mid-fifties, the peoples of Europe felt safe in a way they had never known before in their history. The time had come when daring initiatives were possible. . . .

The Spaak Committee handed in its report to governments on April 23, 1956. It was after that date that the real negotiating began. The ball was set rolling by the Foreign Ministers, who met in Venice on May 29 and 30, 1956. The negotiations continued for nearly a year, until the signing of the treaty on March 25, 1957.

It was in that spring of 1956 that France's reactions to the Spaak report made themselves known, that French officialdom and the leading representatives of industry and agriculture expressed their fears, their hostility towards the common market project. Up to that point no one had thought that a venture of this kind could even take shape on paper, let alone become fact. And suddenly here was a text which, of course, had not been formally accepted by anyone, but whose provisions to a large extent prefigured a possible European customs union. Above all, it became known that certain members of the government, and important ones at that—President of the Council Guy Mollet, Foreign Affairs Minister Christian Pineau—were favorably disposed. There was a small group of "Europeans," namely Jean Monnet, myself and a few others, who were determined that Europe should get over the EDC failure. But the obstacles were enormous. Almost all of them were manifestations of the fear that had seized French business and especially government officialdom at the idea that the wall of protection, of all kinds, built up during the prewar, war and postwar years might one day come down and that French industry would then have to face foreign competition without customs duties, quotas or state subsidies. The very thought made the interested parties feel as helpless as Spartan babes on the mountainside.

As for me, I was delighted. Here at last was a task worth giving one's all to! A successful outcome would mean the start of an era of trading freedom from which France and Europe—the two were inseparable in my mind—would benefit. That it would be necessary to do battle on all fronts, in Brussels against our partners, who found it difficult to agree to certain of France's demands, in Paris against officialdom, which was almost unanimously opposed to the idea of the Common Market, and also against a number of industrial and agricultural lobbies that wanted special advantages, guarantees or additional protection, made the task even more stimulating. Never, since my entry into higher education twenty-five years earlier, did I work so hard. I felt as though I were in the center of a web which would finally encompass the myriad subjects of negotiation and which, fortified by the trust placed in me by Guy Mollet and Christian Pineau, I was helping to weave strand by strand.

French officialdom was the first battlefront. Its stance was entirely negative. . . .

I said earlier that all the countries taking part in the negotiation were behind the Common Market project, *except France*. The problem was therefore to come up with answers to the sensitive issues that would reassure the French without unduly disquieting the other partners. As of a certain moment, a real complicity developed in Brussels between the French delegation and the others in the search for those answers. I can remember certain dinners at which we French, Belgians, Dutch and Germans would tell one another frankly what was acceptable to each of us. I think it was at one of those dinners that, during a conversation with Robert Rothschild and Etienne Davignon, who both held high posts in the Belgian government service, I suggested the drafting of a special text that would help to allay French fears. That was the origin of the "Protocol relating to certain provisions of concern to France," which was annexed to the Treaty.

This protocol allowed France to retain, during such time as the French balance of payments remained in deficit, her special system of export aids and import surcharges. France was thus spared the need to devalue her currency, at least for a time. . . .

Thanks to Adenauer, the problem of association of the overseas countries was settled quite easily. The solution adopted guaranteed that those countries' products would have free access to the Community. As regards exports from Europe, the member countries of the Common Market were placed on an equal footing, the overseas countries being able to go on protecting their nascent industries to a degree. Furthermore, the Common Market countries undertook to contribute to the investment necessary to the progressive development of the overseas countries. It was a simple solution, which continued to be applied when the overseas countries acceded to independence shortly afterwards. France, though she was progressively to lose the preference she enjoyed in her colonies, ultimately came out ahead. She was obliged to seek out other markets, where she would face international competition, and thus to become competitive.

The agricultural problem was more difficult to resolve. A lot of effort had to be expended for several years after the signing of the Treaty in order to frame the common agricultural policy, but the foundations of it had been laid in the Treaty. I have said that the French wanted community agriculture to enjoy a tariff preference, to which a number of our partners, notably the Germans, were opposed for doctrinal reasons. This opposition was all the less justified in that Germany's agriculture, like that of every other member country, was highly protected. All that was needed was to combine each country's protective measures into a community protection, while at the same time establishing free movement of farm goods within the Community, and the common agricultural policy could see the light of day. . . .

. . . But France would never have accepted a customs union that did not include agriculture and did not guarantee French producers protection comparable to that which they were receiving under French law. Without a common agricultural policy there would never have been a Common Market.

The special interest of the farmers weighed heavy in the balance. Moreover, the French government and its services were convinced that the Common Market would primarily benefit German industry, would add still further to its might, which already seemed awesome. The only way to redress the balance was to allow French farmers to export to Germany, where they would be on an equal footing with German farmers. The Germans were ready to accept the French demands. Their agriculture, although limited in scale, had a high protective wall around it. It was difficult for them to refuse, in the name of principles, comparable protection for European agriculture as a whole. Chancellor Adenauer's will to integrate Germany into a European community, thus erasing, as far as was humanly possible, the tragic memories of a war not long past, and in particular his determination to set the seal on Franco-German reconciliation, took care of the rest. . . .

With all the difficulties settled, the treaty establishing the European Economic Community was able to be signed in Rome on March 25, 1957, at the same time as the treaty establishing Euratom.

I do not believe it is an exaggeration to say that this date represents one of the great moments of Europe's history. Who would have thought during the thirties, and even during the ten years that followed the war, that European states which had been tearing one another apart for so many centuries and some of which, like France and Italy, still had very closed economies, would form a common market intended eventually to become an economic area that could be likened to one great domestic market?

As will be seen clearly later on, France, which of all the Common Market countries was the one that most feared this exposure to the outside world, was the one that ultimately derived the greatest benefit. The straitjacket of protectionism was suddenly removed. There may be some question of whether Germany and Benelux really needed the Common Market in order to expand their production capacity as they did; their development might not have been all that different without the Treaty of Rome, given their low tariff levels and the Americans' wish for a worldwide reduction of customs duties. But the evolution of the French economy would certainly have been very different and less favorable, without it being possible to say what course things would finally have taken.

34

PAUL-HENRI SPAAK

Rome Treaty Negotiations as First Stage of a Political Revolution

1956–March 1957

In this excerpt from his memoirs, Spaak described how, as head of the intergovernmental committee, he organized his foreign colleagues to produce the Spaak Report in May 1956. During the next ten months, the committee conducted very difficult negotiations, which nearly failed. It drafted two treaties, one outlining a common market and a customs union, the European Economic Community (EEC), and the other creating the European Atomic Energy Community (Euratom). The treaties, known collectively as the Treaty of Rome, decreed that decisions would be taken by a majority vote in the Council of Ministers and that the principle of equality in voting power applied to small and large nations alike.

I must now revert to the talks which culminated in the drafting of the Treaties of Rome. These negotiations went on for nearly two years, and we repeatedly came close to failure. It was a tremendous task we were facing.

After we had defined our goal at the Messina Conference and issued a number of general directives, we held our first meeting in Brussels in July 1955. The delegation leaders were Ambassador Ophüls for Germany, Baron Snoy for Belgium, Félix Gaillard for France, Ludovico Benvenuti for Italy, Lambert Schaus for Luxembourg and Professor Verryn Stuart for the Netherlands.

I believed in the task we were about to undertake and was most eager to carry it through, and this gave me courage. We did not get off to an easy start. How were we to approach so vast an enterprise?

Paul-Henri Spaak, *The Continuing Battle: Memoirs of a European, 1936–1966* (Boston: Little, Brown, 1971), 238–52. Text of the treaties available at http://eur-lex.europa.eu/en/treaties/index.htm and http://www.ieu.it/.

We began in the classical manner by setting up a number of committees functioning independently. In this way a great deal of material was assembled but little progress made. I was compelled to admit as much to my colleagues when we met at the Dutch resort of Noordwijk in September 1955. They were patient and sympathetic and encouraged me to carry on with the work. I soon made up my mind that a change of method was called for. I realized that if I became ensnared in endless technical discussions without first laying down specific guidelines and taking out certain political options, I should get nowhere. I therefore decided to wind up the committees, while reserving the right to call in the experts again at a later date, and to deal directly with the various heads of delegation.

The delegation leaders all helped me greatly in the task of preparing the ground. Our discussions were often heated, but they enabled us to define our fundamental principles. These, in turn, were to become the basis of the Common Market. The chief problems were listed. When I felt that sufficient progress had been made I sent Pierre Uri, [Hans] von der Groeben and [Albert] Hupperts to the south of France, where they could work in peace. Their job was to draft a report in order to formulate the conclusions at which we had arrived during our discussions. This proved an excellent method. The draft they prepared—a task so difficult that it would probably have proved unmanageable had it been left to the six heads of delegation—was accepted as largely correct. It was discussed point by point, and the text finally adopted did not depart from the original draft either in general content or style. This is how the document eventually to be known as the "Spaak Report" came into being. . . .

The essential feature of this work is the fundamental choice it reflects. There were two alternatives before us: we could establish a simple customs union or a common market. We decided to go for the bolder of these two courses. The report defined what was meant by the common market we had in mind, and it did so, not in vague, general terms but by setting out the various problems that would have to be tackled, the difficulties that would have to be overcome, and by defining in advance the answers to these questions.

Compared with the communiqué issued after the Messina Conference, the progress accomplished on this occasion was considerable. The ideas which had only been outlined vaguely at Messina were this time listed, defined and explained. The governments were now in a position to assess accurately the implications of a policy which they had up to now endorsed in principle only.

The report also contained a chapter dealing with the creation of an "atomic community." We had been helped tremendously in this work by Louis Armand,[1] who may rightly claim to be the father of Euratom. . . .

The "Spaak Report" was discussed by the foreign ministers in Venice on 29 and 30 May 1956. Baron Snoy was right in calling this the "miraculous conference." Never before had agreement on questions of such importance been reached so swiftly. The document on which we based our negotiations had been distributed, read and carefully analyzed in advance. There was no need for me to explain or to defend it. Agreement was general. In less than two hours, the six partners decided that the document should be adopted as the basis for our future negotiations. Having thus proved all the pessimists wrong, we entered upon a new stage in our work.

A fresh conference was due to open in Brussels on 26 June and, at Pineau's suggestion, I was asked to carry on with my task of giving encouragement to the others involved in this work and coordinating their activities. Our job on this occasion was to draft two treaties—the one which established the Common Market, and the Euratom agreement. To complete our task, we were bound to have much to discuss, for, as our ideas crystallized, new difficulties and clashes of interest emerged. Several months were necessary to see this work through to its conclusion. It was a harassing task, but I found the work fascinating and shall never forget it. It is not often one can say to oneself that one is expending one's energies to ensure the triumph of a great ideal. . . .

These were some of the minor ups and downs in what were essentially very serious discussions. Moments of crisis occurred in the negotiations when we had to deal with such matters as the military uses of uranium, when France announced the conditions she considered indispensable in this context, and when we had to settle the fate of the former colonies. This list should in itself suffice to show that our problems were essentially political. . . .

In a speech which was listened to with rapt attention, Maurice Faure enumerated all the questions which the French Government would wish to see solved first, as well as all the guarantees he felt to be essential. It was a long and impressive list. Its principal items were: harmonization of social legislation; France's continued right to subsidize

[1]Head of French nationalized railways and chairman of the Euratom working group on the intergovernmental committee.

certain types of exports; her right to maintain a surcharge on imports and, finally, the inclusion of overseas territories in the Common Market. Another French proposal was that there should be no fixed timetable for the establishment of the Common Market by stages; instead, the introduction of each successive stage should be subject to the attainment, one by one, of specific objectives defined in advance.

As Maurice Faure went on with his speech I could see the faces of the other delegates growing longer and longer. Although I recognized that there was a good deal of justice in the French requests, I realized how difficult their acceptance was bound to be. Because of their very extent, there was a danger that these requests would be rejected out of hand. . . .

Finally, the last few obstacles were overcome and soon the only problem remaining was that of the association of the overseas territories with the Common Market. At this point it became necessary to call a meeting of the Heads of Government. It was held in Paris on 18 and 19 February 1957. Though the financial implications were important, the political and psychological aspects were even more vital. The Italians and Germans, who after the two world wars had been stripped of their colonies, some of which now belonged to their new partners, were to be asked to contribute to development schemes drawn up by the new owners of these territories. This was not an easy concession for the Germans and Italians to make. The resistance of the Germans, supported by the Dutch, had proved impossible to overcome at the heads of delegation level. The difference, therefore, became a matter for the governments to settle and hence the prime ministers were bound to intervene. They all gathered in Paris—Adenauer, Guy Mollet, Segni, van Acker, [Joseph] Bech and Drees—assisted by their Foreign Ministers—von Brentano, [Christian] Pineau and Maurice Faure, Martino, Luns and myself.[2] A debate of epic proportions ensued. It went on day and night. I had to go from delegate to delegate, pleading and looking for compromise solutions. Finally, in the small hours of 20 February, a solution was found. Once again it was Adenauer who showed himself to be a true statesman. Germany's contribution, it was decided, was to be equal to that of France, and yet it was the territories associated with the latter which stood to gain most from the new arrangements. . . .

[2]Antonio Segni, Italian prime minister; Achille van Acker, Belgian prime minister; Willem Drees, Dutch prime minister; Heinrich von Brentano, German foreign minister; Gaetano Martino, Italian foreign minister; Joseph Luns, Dutch foreign minister.

It is not my intention at this time to discuss the treaty in detail. All I wish to do now is to recall some of its outstanding features. I am thinking, above all, of its supranational character. There has been a great deal of talk about this particular aspect of it—an essential feature inasmuch as it implies the abandonment of the absurd rule of unanimity. This rule, which requires that all decisions be taken unanimously, is the plague of international organizations and the cause of their partial paralysis. Since its application would be inconceivable in the internal life of the nations, one wonders why it should be applied in international affairs. No organization can function without power, nor can it work if the will—and sometimes the ill-will—of a single member can nullify the will of the rest.

The rule of unanimity was responsible for the bankruptcy of the League of Nations. The right of veto—a watered-down version of the same principle—has rendered the UN Security Council powerless. It has also enabled General de Gaulle to provoke crises of the utmost gravity in the European Community itself.

The authors of the Treaty of Rome were aware of these dangers. They held that the will of the majority should as a rule prevail and that unanimous decisions should only be mandatory in exceptional circumstances. This was a major advance, the importance of which was further enhanced by the application of the "weighted vote."

The equality of states is a purely academic concept. To say, as is being said in the UN, that the vote of the smallest Powers must carry the same weight as that of the greatest is to fly in the face of reality. The only way to make the Great Powers surrender the right of veto is to apply a system which would give their vote an importance in line with their real status.

After laborious discussions, we succeeded in having these principles incorporated in the Common Market treaty. . . .

On 25 March 1957 we signed two treaties in Rome which established, respectively, the Common Market and Euratom. It was an unforgettable ceremony, which the Italians had organized in the grand manner. We met in the Capitol, and all the chief architects of the great enterprise whose completion we were formally to record were there: the ministers who had supplied the initial impulse; the heads of delegation, who had done a tremendous job, as well as the experts who had aided us all. The bells of Rome rang out to salute the birth of the new Europe. My own heart was full of joy, emotion and hope, and I made a speech which reflected my feelings.

The Treaty of Rome symbolizes the triumph of the spirit of cooperation over national selfishness. Those who had brought the exercise to a successful conclusion were inspired by the same convictions and the same ideals. They were aware of the economic changes they had brought about. But however great these changes might be, so far as the architects of the Common Market were concerned, they were of secondary importance or, at any rate, only the first stage of an even more important revolution which was still to come—a political revolution.

Ten years later this ideal remains as valid as it was then. It is the only ideal which does justice to our age, the only ideal capable of restoring Europe to her rightful place, a place to which she is entitled by virtue of her illustrious past.

4

De Gaulle, the European Economic Community, and the French-German Treaty

35

CHARLES DE GAULLE

A Europe of States

May 15, 1962

In a press conference promoting his initiative, the Fouchet Plan, a new European organization outside the EEC and NATO (which EEC leaders rejected), French president Charles de Gaulle stressed the importance of the nation-states as the pillars on which Europe could be built. He continually argued for a concert of European states, a system based on cooperation between states. Part of de Gaulle's press conference is reprinted here.

In the French view, this economic construction [of Europe] is not enough. Western Europe—whether it be a matter of its actions vis-à-vis other people, of its own defense, of its contribution to the development of regions that are in need of it, or of its duty to European balance and international détente—Western Europe must form itself politically. Moreover, if it did not succeed in doing so, the European Community itself could not in the long run become stronger or even continue to exist. In other words, Europe must have institutions that will lead it to form a political union, just as it is already a union in the economic sphere. . . .

Major Addresses, Statements, and Press Conferences of General Charles de Gaulle, May 19, 1958–January 31, 1964 (New York: French Embassy Press and Information Bureau, 1964), 176.

What is it that France is proposing to her five partners? I shall repeat it once again: To organize ourselves politically, let us begin at the beginning. Let us organize our cooperation, let our Heads of State or of Government meet periodically to examine our problems together and to make decisions with regard to these problems which will be the decisions of Europe. Let us set up a political commission, a defense commission, and a cultural commission, just as we have already formed an economic commission in Brussels which studies common questions and prepares the decisions of the six Governments. Naturally, the political commission and the others will proceed, in this regard, in conditions that are appropriate to their particular domains. Moreover, the Ministers in charge of these various fields will meet whenever necessary to implement in concert the decisions that will be taken by the [European] Council. Finally, we have a European parliamentary assembly that meets in Strasbourg and is composed of delegations from our six national Parliaments. Let us enable this assembly to discuss common political questions as it already discusses economic questions. After we have tried it, we shall see, in three years' time, what we can do to strengthen our ties.

. . . It is true that the nation is a human and sentimental element, whereas Europe can be built on the basis of active, authoritative, and responsible elements. What elements? The State, of course; for in this respect, it is only the States that are valid, legitimate, and capable of achievement. I have already said, and I repeat, that at the present time there cannot be any other Europe than a Europe of States, apart, of course, from myths, stories, and parades. What is happening with regard to the [European] Economic Community proves this every day, for it is the States, and only the States, that created this Economic Community . . . and it is the States that give it reality and efficiency.

36

JOHN F. KENNEDY

Declaration of Interdependence Speech

July 4, 1962

In Philadelphia on Independence Day, President John Kennedy outlined his "Grand Design," his approach to European affairs. This meant that in foreign policy, he accorded top priority to Europe and ardently supported European unity because he knew it was key to America's success, security, and survival. This excerpt from Kennedy's speech demonstrates his view of the United States and a strong, united Europe as partners, not rivals. He spoke about this Atlantic partnership as two pillars of democracy of equal weight, with leaders of equal voice.

In most of the old colonial world, the struggle for independence is coming to an end. Even in areas behind the [Iron] Curtain, that which Jefferson called "the disease of liberty" still appears to be infectious. With the passing of ancient empires, today less than 2 percent of the world's population lives in territories officially termed "dependent." As this effort for independence, inspired by the American Declaration of Independence, now approaches a successful close, a great new effort—for interdependence—is transforming the world about us. And the spirit of that new effort is the same spirit which gave birth to the American Constitution.

That spirit is today most clearly seen across the Atlantic Ocean. The nations of Western Europe, long divided by feuds far more bitter than any which existed among the 13 colonies, are today joining together, seeking, as our forefathers sought, to find freedom in diversity and in unity, strength.

The United States looks on this vast new enterprise with hope and admiration. We do not regard a strong and united Europe as a rival but as a partner. To aid its progress has been the basic object of our

---

John F. Kennedy, *Public Papers of the Presidents of the United States: John F. Kennedy, 1962* (Washington, D.C.: Government Printing Office, 1967), 537–39.

foreign policy for 17 years. We believe that a united Europe will be capable of playing a greater role in the common defense, of responding more generously to the needs of poorer nations, of joining with the United States and others in lowering trade barriers, resolving problems of commerce, commodities, and currency, and developing coordinated policies in all economic, political, and diplomatic areas. We see in such a Europe a partner with whom we can deal on a basis of full equality in all the great and burdensome tasks of building and defending a community of free nations.

It would be premature at this time to do more than indicate the high regard with which we view the formation of this partnership. The first order of business is for our European friends to go forward in forming the more perfect union which will someday make this partnership possible.

A great new edifice is not built overnight. It was 11 years from the Declaration of Independence to the writing of the Constitution. The construction of workable federal institutions required still another generation. The greatest works of our Nation's founders lay not in documents and in declarations, but in creative, determined action. The building of the new house of Europe has followed the same practical, purposeful course. Building the Atlantic partnership now will not be easily or cheaply finished.

But I will say here and now, on this Day of Independence, that the United States will be ready for a Declaration of Interdependence, that we will be prepared to discuss with a united Europe the ways and means of forming a concrete Atlantic partnership, a mutually beneficial partnership between the new union now emerging in Europe and the old American Union founded here 175 years ago.

All this will not be completed in a year, but let the world know it is our goal.

In urging the adoption of the United States Constitution, Alexander Hamilton told his fellow New Yorkers "to think continentally." Today Americans must learn to think intercontinentally.

Acting on our own, by ourselves, we cannot establish justice throughout the world; we cannot insure its domestic tranquility, or provide for its common defense, or promote its general welfare, or secure the blessings of liberty to ourselves and our posterity. But joined with other free nations, we can do all this and more. We can assist the developing nations to throw off the yoke of poverty. We can balance our worldwide trade and payments at the highest possible level of growth. We can mount a deterrent powerful enough to deter any aggression. And ultimately we can help to achieve a world of law and free choice, banishing the world of war and coercion.

For the Atlantic partnership of which I speak would not look inward only, preoccupied with its own welfare and advancement. It must look outward to cooperate with all nations in meeting their common concern. It would serve as a nucleus for the eventual union of all free men—those who are now free and those who are vowing that someday they will be free.

37

HAROLD MACMILLAN

Britain's Decision to Join the European Economic Community

September 10, 1962

British prime minister Harold Macmillan explained his government's decision to apply for membership in the EEC in his September 1962 speech, excerpted here, to the Commonwealth Prime Ministers Conference. Although the economic arguments predominated, he stressed that Britain's membership would add stability to the EEC and Europe and increase his nation's political influence in the world.

On the economic side, Britain's value to the Commonwealth lies in the markets which she offers and in the capital which she provides. By ourselves we cannot increase our market except gradually through the increases in our population—and they are small. If we are to offer you better markets we must therefore increase our wealth. I believe that the prospects of our doing so inside the European Economic Community are better than if we stayed outside. I also believe that our influence and position in Europe will help to secure for the Common-

---

Harold Macmillan, *At the End of the Day, 1961–1963* (New York: Harper & Row, 1973), 537–39.

wealth economic opportunities inside the Community which would otherwise be denied or restricted. On the political side the Community may of course break up—it is possible—or it may grow stronger. If it did collapse the situation would be most dangerous to us all. The economic dislocation would be harmful to world trade; the political consequences would be no less serious. The old rivalries and struggles would very likely begin again and Europe might well succumb to Soviet power which would then perhaps reach to the very Straits of Dover. So we desire to see the forces of unity in Europe grow stronger and banish for ever the fear of a return of the quarrels and destruction of the past. We believe that British membership of the Community would lend a new element of stability to it. . . . As members both of the Commonwealth and of Europe, we are bound to have a special responsibility. We cannot refuse the great opportunity of playing our full part in the movement, slow or rapid as it may be, towards the ultimate world order into which mankind must move or perish.

38

CHARLES DE GAULLE

Veto of British Application for EEC Membership

January 14, 1963

At a press conference, excerpted here, French president de Gaulle vetoed Britain's application to the European Economic Community. He claimed that Britain's close relationship with the United States threatened Europe with American domination. He also declared his categorical refusal to subscribe to the Nassau Accords, an agreement concluded in December 1962 whereby the United States would supply Polaris missiles to Britain. A similar offer had been made to France, which carried membership in NATO's proposed multilateral force. (The U.S. proposal, which never materialized, offered Western Europeans an opportunity to help man and pay for nuclear forces primarily under U.S. control. Its

Major Addresses, Statements, and Press Conferences of General Charles de Gaulle, May 19, 1958–January 31, 1964 (New York: French Embassy Press and Information Bureau, 1964), 213–19.

purpose was to prevent the creation of more national nuclear forces in Europe, especially the emergence of a separate German nuclear force, and to deflect the feeling among Europeans that they were not participants in their own defense.) De Gaulle's refusal gave him another opportunity to dramatize his anti-American stance and justify his plan to pursue the development of an independent nuclear deterrent.

Then Great Britain applied for membership in the Common Market. It did so after refusing earlier to participate in the community that was being built, and after then having created a free trade area with six other States, and finally . . . after having put some pressure on the Six in order to prevent the application of the Common Market from really getting started. Britain thus in turn requested membership, but on its own conditions.

This undoubtedly raises for each of the six States and for England problems of a very great dimension.

England is, in effect, insular, maritime, linked through its trade, markets, and food supply to very diverse and often very distant countries. Its activities are essentially industrial and commercial, and only slightly agricultural. It has . . . very marked and original customs and traditions. In short, the nature, structure, and economic context of England differ profoundly from those of the other States of the Continent. . . .

One was sometimes led to believe that our British friends, in applying for membership in the Common Market, agreed to change their own ways even to the point of applying all the conditions accepted and practiced by the Six, but the question is to know if Great Britain can at present place itself, with the Continent and like it, within a tariff that is truly common, give up all preference with regard to the Commonwealth, cease to claim that its agriculture be privileged, and even more, consider as null and void the commitments it has made with the countries that are part of its free trade area. That question is the one at issue.

One cannot say that it has now been resolved. Will it be so one day? Obviously, only Britain can answer that.

The question is raised all the more since, following Britain, other States which are, I repeat, linked to it in the Free Trade Area, for the same reasons as Great Britain, would or will want to enter the Common Market.

It must be agreed that the entry first of Great Britain and then of those other States will completely change the series of adjustments, agreements, compensations, and regulations already established between the Six, because all these States, like Britain, have very important traits of their own. We would then have to envisage the construction of another Common Market. But the 11-member, then 13-member, and then perhaps 18-member Common Market that would be built would, without any doubt, hardly resemble the one the Six have built.

Moreover, this Community, growing in that way, would be confronted with all the problems of its economic relations with a crowd of other States, and first of all with the United States.

It is foreseeable that the cohesion of all its members, who would be very numerous and very diverse, would not hold for long and that in the end there would appear a colossal Atlantic Community under American dependence and leadership which would soon completely swallow up the European Community.

This is an assumption that can be perfectly justified in the eyes of some, but it is not at all what France wanted to do and what France is doing, which is a strictly European construction.

39

CHARLES DE GAULLE AND KONRAD ADENAUER

Common Declaration of the French-German Treaty

January 22, 1963

Eight days after rejecting Britain's application for EEC membership, de Gaulle signed the French-German Treaty of Friendship and Reconciliation, excerpted here, with West German chancellor Konrad Adenauer at the Elysée Palace in Paris. This historic and critical step in the process of reconciliation between two rival powers strengthened integration. In

Reprinted from an unofficial translation issued by the French Embassy Press and Information Service, New York. See also George W. Ball, *The Past Has Another Pattern: Memoirs* (New York: W. W. Norton, 1982), 271–72.

April 1963, however, the German Bundestag undermined the French-German exclusiveness embodied in this treaty by revising the preamble and stating that the treaty did not supersede Germany's existing international agreements, including NATO and General Agreement on Tariffs and Trade (GATT), signed in 1947. George Ball, undersecretary of state in the Kennedy administration, described the adverse U.S. reaction to the treaty in his memoirs. "I can hardly overestimate the shock produced in Washington by this action or speculation that followed," he wrote. The American government feared a "Paris-Bonn deal with Moscow" leading to a possible Soviet withdrawal from East Germany, "followed by some form of confederation between the two parts of that severed country." That would mean "the end of NATO and the neutralization of Germany." According to Ball, Washington feared that if the United States and Western Europe made separate demands or took conflicting approaches to the Soviet Union, Moscow "would play one off against the other. That would mean the disintegration of our common security."

Convinced that the reconciliation of the German people and the French people, bringing an end to the age-old rivalries, constitutes a historic event which profoundly transforms the relations of the two peoples,

Conscious of the solidarity which unites the two peoples both with respect to their security and with respect to their economic and cultural development,

Observing particularly that young people have become aware of this solidarity and find themselves called upon to play the determinant role in the consolidation of French-German friendship,

Recognizing that a strengthening of the cooperation between the two countries constitutes a vital stage along the road to a united Europe, which is the goal of the two peoples,

Have agreed to the organization and to the principles of the cooperation between the two States as they are stated in the Treaty signed this day.

Done at Paris, on the twenty-second day of January in the year one thousand nine hundred and sixty-three, in both the French and German languages.

40

JOHN F. KENNEDY

"We Have to Live with de Gaulle"

January 22, 1963

This excerpt from a summary of the U.S. National Security Council meeting on January 22, 1963, reveals President Kennedy's irritation with de Gaulle's anti-American policies. Kennedy noted that despite de Gaulle's opposition to Britain's membership in the EEC and U.S. efforts to strengthen NATO, the French president did not question American support for Europe and remained dependent on the United States for his nation's security. Kennedy asserted that in the forthcoming trade negotiations with Europe, U.S. economic interests must be protected.

Turning to Europe, the President recalled that de Gaulle's current policy is no different from what he has been advocating since 1958 when he first proposed to President Eisenhower a U.S.-U.K.-France directorate giving France, in effect, a veto on our use of nuclear weapons.[1] The suggestion was turned down because it would have broken up NATO. This Administration agrees it was a correct decision. The turndown of de Gaulle's proposal was not, however, the reason why he is behaving as he now is. Even if we had given France nuclear weapons, de Gaulle would have tried to restore France to a predominant position in Europe. For years, in speeches and in his memoirs, de Gaulle has expressed his view that France must be a dominant power speaking to the USSR and the West as an equal, dependent on no one.

In analyzing de Gaulle's present actions, the President said de Gaulle did not question our support of Europe. The proof that he does not fear we would desert him is the deployment of only a small number of French troops opposite the Russians in Germany. He relies on our power to protect him while he launches his policies based solely on the self-interest of France. Having been turned down by the U.S.

[1]In September 1958, de Gaulle had proposed that these three nations form a tripartite directorate for global policy.

Foreign Relations of the United States, 1961–1963, VIII, 457–62.

and U.K. on the directorate, de Gaulle turned to Germany.[2] This helps to keep Germany from looking to the Russians. It does threaten NATO which de Gaulle strongly opposes.

As to the Common Market, the President said that if Great Britain joined, Europe would be strengthened and stabilized. We favor the U.K. joining even though it will cost the U.S. considerable trade. If France keeps Britain out, this will be a setback for us but a more severe setback for the U.K.

Our interest, the President continued, is to strengthen the NATO multilateral force concept, even though de Gaulle is opposed, because a multilateral force will increase our influence in Europe and provide a way to guide NATO and keep it strong. We have to live with de Gaulle. One way to respond is to strengthen NATO and push for a multilateral nuclear force which will weaken de Gaulle's control of the Six. We should not be overly distressed because the problems caused by de Gaulle are not crucial in the sense that our problems in Latin America are.

The President then summarized the guidelines for forthcoming trade negotiations. In the present situation, we must be very careful to protect U.S. interests. Our balance of payments problem is serious, it is not now under control, and it must be righted at the latest by the end of 1964. If we do not do so, there will be pressure against the dollar and Congress will be demanding reductions on our foreign programs.

One effort we must make, the President continued, is to seek to prevent European states from taking actions which make our balance of payments problem worse. For example, we maintain large forces in Germany. We must firmly oppose West Germany if it increases its agricultural production to our detriment. We have not yet reached the point of wheat against troops but we cannot continue to pay for the military protection of Europe while the NATO states are not paying their fair share and living off the "fat of the land." We have been very generous to Europe and it is now time for us to look out for ourselves, knowing full well that the Europeans will not do anything for us simply because we have in the past helped them. No longer dependent on the U.S. for economic assistance, the European states are less subject to our influence. If the French and other European powers acquire a nuclear capability they would be in a position to be entirely

[2]French-German Treaty of Friendship and Reconciliation, January 22, 1963 (Document 39).

independent and we might be on the outside looking in. We must exploit our military and political position to ensure that our economic interests are protected.

41

WALTER HALLSTEIN

"The European Community . . . Is a Process of Continuous Creation"

March 2, 1963

In a speech at Columbia University in New York, the first president of the EEC's Commission, West German government official Walter Hallstein, explained that European integration was "dynamic" in character. What was being achieved, he declared, was political union in the economic field. Part of Hallstein's speech is reprinted here.

I should like to focus upon the European Community [in] the light cast by the present crisis,[1] which in many respects throws the Community's contours into sharper relief. In particular, I believe that that light reveals its dynamic character. For the European Community is not something static, or something readymade; it is a process of continuous creation. It is a policy, an endless series of questions and answers, of continual challenges and responses. . . .

The fundamental change that the European Community represented, therefore, was a reorientation of European politics. That is why Great Britain's application for membership in the Community was such a remarkable sign that her own fundamental attitudes had been transformed. In the past, Britain had played an honorable and often valuable role in helping to maintain the balance of power. In the early

[1]De Gaulle's veto of Britain's application for EEC membership, January 14, 1963 (Document 38).

Walter Hallstein, "The European Community," *Political Science Quarterly*, 78, no. 2 (Summer 1963): 161–78.

postwar years her reaction to those bids for European unity that went beyond mere cooperation had been hesitant, to say the least. Now, her government had put all hesitation behind it. In place of the balance of power, it was prepared to accept the fusion of interests, the pooling of resources and problems, and full participation in the great task of unity.

This was a very profound change, and like all such changes, it was profoundly difficult. The difficulty was increased, moreover, by a second political aspect of the Community which again the negotiations helped to make clear. I have said that the Community represents the fusion of interests, but a further important characteristic is that that fusion is progressive.

By its very nature, therefore, the European Community must be an ever-growing, ever-developing organism. And this, of course, makes negotiation with it extremely difficult. . . .

This last question again is a theme for Atlantic Partnership, for here, too, the emergence of a united Europe means the emergence of a partner who should be able to help the United States bear a burden whose weight is known and acknowledged everywhere. Nor is it only a burden in the financial sense. It is also an intellectual challenge to us to solve by our joint efforts the problems of the "terms of trade." . . .

True, we face obstacles. But if we can define their limits as I have tried to do, we may find that they have clarified our ideas and strengthened our resolve. And if there is one conclusion that I draw from the events of recent weeks, it is this: we need the European Community. We need it for Great Britain, for if she is one day to join it, there must be a Community for her to join. We need it for Europe, to replace an outworn system that has brought only disaster and ruin. Finally, we need it for the free world, as one pillar of the Atlantic Partnership that is the sole guarantee of our own continued freedom and the world's continued peace.

42

KONRAD ADENAUER

Without French-German Reconciliation, "Europe Is Unthinkable"

July 2, 1963

In a conversation with German journalists, excerpted here, Konrad Adenauer credited the Schuman Plan and the creation of the European Coal and Steel Community as an important step in the reconciliation between France and Germany. Without the ECSC, he said, Europe would not have been created.

Gentlemen, if we think back to the first years after 1945, after our collapse, then you will remember how Russia and France quite seriously aired the idea not to allow a central power to arise in Germany, to divide up this Germany into a series of pieces. Might I also remind you that, then, the plan to internationalize the industrial region—coal still meant something at that time—was aired, and that precisely Russia and France pushed for this internationalization. Then you will concede that I am right [to say]: without reconciliation with France, Europe is unthinkable.

That was the thought of Robert Schuman—whom one cannot mention often enough in this context—as he suggested the coal and steel union. At that time he wrote me a private letter, alongside the official one, in which he said: we have great anxiety about and great mistrust towards Germany when it has recovered. Our people fear that Germany will then revenge itself on France. Thus, he wrote in the letter, armament shows itself first of all through coal production and the production of iron and steel, which are indeed connected. Therefore, if we, he continued, create an institution which makes it possible for one people to observe a sudden increase of the production of iron and

---

"Record of a Conversation between Konrad Adenauer and German Journalists, 2 July, 1963," from *Adenauer: Teegesprache, 1961–63*, Hans-Peter Mensing, ed., in *The Origins and Development of European Integration*, ed. Peter Stirk and David Weigall (London: Pinter, 1999), 92.

steel by another, and vice-versa, then that is the best means to set aside mutual mistrust.

I tell you this in such detail, gentlemen, so that you will see what the origins of this co-operation of France and Germany were in general and that then, naturally, great anxiety prevailed in France about what might happen between the Germans and the French as things developed. If you consider that, gentlemen, you will agree with me, I believe, that without this reconciliation between France and Germany, Europe would not have been created.

Glossary of Acronyms and Terms

Atlantic community A general term describing the nations of Western Europe, Canada, and the United States; often used as a synonym for NATO.

Benelux Both an acronym for Belgium, the Netherlands, and Luxembourg and the name of a customs union among the three countries that went into effect in 1948.

Cartel An organization of industrial or commercial producers of a commodity, such as coal or oil, that have united to control prices and regulate output.

Common agricultural policy (CAP) The farm policy of the EEC, involving a complicated set of price supports and subsidies as outlined in Article 39 of the Rome Treaty. The CAP stipulated that member states establish a common agricultural policy with the following objectives: increase agricultural productivity, ensure a fair standard of living for those engaged in its production, stabilize markets, ensure the availability of supplies, and ensure reasonable prices for consumers. The members agreed in 1962 to establish a single market in agriculture based on guaranteed common prices, preferential treatment for EEC products (which meant levies on imports), and subsidized exports. The cost of this policy was to be shared by its members.

Common market The result of an agreement among a group of countries to integrate their economies beyond a customs union. The group functions as a single economic entity for the purpose of trade and eliminates or markedly reduces all trade barriers and quantitative restrictions to the free movement of goods, services, capital, and labor within the unit's boundaries. The group agrees to levy a common external tariff on imports from outside the group.

Commonwealth of Nations An association or federation of autonomous states. The British Commonwealth of Nations, later known as the Commonwealth, was created by Great Britain in 1931 to maintain close relations, especially in trade, with its former colonies and included self-governing states as well as dependencies.

Confederal Pertaining to a confederation.

Confederation A group or union of independent states or nations working together toward a common goal. Less binding than a federation, the states in a confederation would, in principle, not lose their separate identities and would retain the right of secession.

Customs union A group of states that agree to reduce or eliminate tariffs or barriers to trade with each other and to adopt a common external tariff of customs duties on imports in order to enable goods (but not labor or capital) to move freely within the union.

Direct elections The method by which voters directly elect representatives to a governing body. Beginning in 1979, representatives to the European Parliament were directly elected. Previously, governments most often selected members from their national parliaments to serve in the European Parliament.

Economic Cooperation Act Also called the Foreign Assistance Act of 1948. This bill, passed by Congress and signed by President Truman on April 1, 1948, embodied the Marshall Plan, or the European Recovery Program, as it was formally called.

EEC, EC, EU **EEC** (European Economic Community) applies to the period from 1957 to 1967. **EC** (European Communities or Community) came into use in 1967, when the Merger Treaty, signed on April 8, 1965, and entered into force in 1967, merged the executive bodies of the three communities ECSC, EEC, and Euratom. **EU** (European Union) stems from the Treaty on European Union (TEU), also called the Maastricht Treaty, signed on February 7, 1992, and entered into force in 1993. At that time, the EC was brought under the umbrella of EU. Most scholars use either EC or EU to refer to events from 1957 on.

European Atomic Energy Community (Euratom) An institution created by the Treaties of Rome of March 25, 1957, wherein the six nations agreed to promote the peaceful uses of atomic energy and further the cause of European integration.

European Coal and Steel Community (ECSC) A supranational economic community created by the Treaty of Paris of April 18, 1951; established a six-nation common market in coal and steel.

European Defense Community (EDC) The supranational defense community embodied in a treaty signed on May 27, 1952. This controversial plan was never ratified by all six ECSC nations and therefore was never established.

European Economic Community (EEC) A regional international organization created by the Treaties of Rome of March 25, 1957. Six Western European nations agreed to establish a customs union and eventually a common market.

European Free Trade Association (EFTA) An organization created at Britain's initiative by the Stockholm Convention in January 1960 to establish a free trade area. Six nations joined Britain—Austria, Denmark, Norway, Portugal, Sweden, and Switzerland.

Federal A form of government constituted by a compact between political units or nations that surrender sovereignty in some areas but retain other powers.

Federalism A form of government in which power is constitutionally divided between different territorial levels and units in such a way that each exercises responsibility for a particular set of functions; the distribution of power in an organization, such as a government, between the central authority and the constituent units.

Federation A federal government; a union of units, organizations, or states.

Free trade area A group of countries pledged to remove barriers to mutual trade but not to the movement of labor or capital. Each member determines its own commercial relations with nonmembers but agrees to rules of origin, which set the terms by which goods manufactured outside the area may move from one state to another within it.

Intergovernmental Existing or occurring between two or more national governments. In the EU, intergovernmentalism was epitomized by the system of decision making in the Council of Ministers (before the widespread use of qualified majority voting) whereby each nation had a vote and a veto and decisions had to be unanimous, thereby protecting members' core national interests.

League of Nations An international organization founded in 1919, after the First World War, in an effort to prevent war through collective security and to settle disputes through negotiation.

Nation A body of people associated with an identifiable geographical territory. These people usually share a common culture, history, and language or languages. A nation is distinct from a state (a political concept) and may include people of disparate historic traditions.

Nationalism National spirit or aspiration; devotion to the interests of one's nation.

Nation-state A political unit consisting of an autonomous state inhabited predominantly by a people or cluster of groups sharing a common culture, history, and language.

North Atlantic Treaty Organization (NATO) Known as the Atlantic alliance, a defensive alliance created by the North Atlantic Treaty signed on April 4, 1949, by ten Western European countries, the United States, and Canada.

Organization for European Economic Cooperation (OEEC) An organization established in April 1948, at the insistence of the U.S. government, to channel Marshall Plan assistance to the sixteen recipient countries in Western Europe. The representatives of these nations were charged with identifying a method of allocating aid to each member and coordinating their economic activities.

Qualified majority voting (QMV) A voting procedure, stipulated in the Treaty of Rome but not widely used until the late 1980s, governing decision making in the Council of Ministers. QMV involves weighted voting, whereby each state is allocated a certain number of votes based on its population size, with Germany and France having equal representation. A qualified majority usually amounts to about 70 percent of the total votes in the council. Decisions requiring a qualified majority to pass generally favor the less populous states, which are relatively overrepresented in the allocation of votes.

Referendum The principle or procedure of referring or submitting measures already passed by the legislative body to the vote of the electorate for approval or rejection.

Sector One unit or industry in an economy, such as the agricultural sector or the steelmaking sector.

Sectoral Pertaining to a sector.

Sectoral supranational community A supranational organization with authority over one sector or industry. Decisions are made by majority vote; the power of one nation to block a decision by a veto is eliminated.

Social Democratic party (SPD) A political party in West Germany.

Social Market Economy The main economic model used in Western and Northern Europe in the postwar period, it seeks a middle path between democratic socialism and American-style liberal capitalism, i.e., a mixed economy. It aims at maintaining a balance, through state intervention, between a high rate of economic growth, low inflation, low levels of unemployment and good working conditions, protective social policies for workers, and a strong welfare system.

Supranational Transcending national interests, boundaries, or authority.

Transatlantic Extending across the Atlantic Ocean; refers to policies or ideas shared by Western Europe, Canada, and the United States.

Transnational Extending beyond or across national borders or boundaries.

Treaty of Brussels Formally the Treaty of Economic, Social, and Cultural Collaboration and Collective Self-Defense, a mutual defense agreement signed by Britain, France, Belgium, the Netherlands, and Luxembourg on March 17, 1948.

United Nations (UN) A voluntary international organization of states established in 1945 to maintain international peace and security.

Western European Union (WEU) An organization for defense cooperation established on October 23, 1954, when the Treaty of Brussels was amended and enlarged to include West Germany and Italy.

Glossary of Key People

Adenauer, Konrad West German chancellor, 1949–1963.

Aron, Raymond Twentieth-century French writer, political commentator, sociologist, philosopher, and journalist.

Bech, Joseph Luxembourg prime minister, 1926–1937, 1953–1958; presided over Messina Conference.

Bevin, Ernest British foreign minister, 1945–1951.

Beyen, Johan Willem Dutch foreign minister, 1952–1956.

Bidault, Georges French foreign minister, 1947–1948, 1953–1954; prime minister, 1949–1950; defense minister, 1951–1952.

Briand, Aristide French prime minister, 1909–1911, 1913, 1915–1917, 1921–1922; foreign minister, 1925–1932.

Churchill, Winston British prime minister, 1940–1945, 1951–1955; head of Conservative party and leader of the Opposition, 1945–1951.

De Gasperi, Alcide Italian prime minister, 1945–1953.

de Gaulle, Charles Head of French provisional government, 1944–1946; French president, 1958–1969.

Delors, Jacques President of European Commission, 1985–1995.

Dulles, John Foster U.S. secretary of state, 1953–1959.

Eden, Anthony British foreign secretary, 1935–1938, 1940–1945, 1951–1955; prime minister, 1955–1957.

Eisenhower, Dwight Supreme Commander of Allied forces in Europe, 1942–1945; U.S. Army chief of staff, 1945–1948; NATO Supreme Allied Commander in Europe, 1951–1952; U.S. president, 1953–1961.

Erhard, Ludwig West German economics minister, 1949–1963.

Faure, Edgar French prime minister, 1952, 1955–1956; finance and economic minister, 1953–1954.

Faure, Maurice French secretary of state for foreign affairs, 1956–1958.

Gorbachev, Mikhail President and general secretary of the Communist party of the Soviet Union, 1985–1991.

Hallstein, Walter West German Foreign Office's secretary of state, 1951–1958; head of German delegation to Schuman Plan negotiations, 1950–1951; first president of Commission of the EEC, 1958–1967.

Hirsch, Etienne French industrial engineer; member of Planning Commission of Monnet Plan, 1946–1952 and its deputy commissioner, 1949–1952; president of Euratom, 1959–1962.

Hupperts, Albert Belgian diplomat; drafter of Treaties of Rome, 1956–1957.

Kennedy, John F. U.S. president, 1961–1963.

Kohl, Helmut West German (and later German) chancellor, 1982–1998.

Kohnstamm, Max Dutch Foreign Office official, 1948–1952; head of Secretariat of ECSC High Authority, 1952–1955; secretary-general of Action Committee for the United States of Europe, 1956–1975.

Macmillan, Harold British foreign secretary, 1955; prime minister, 1957–1963.

Marjolin, Robert French political economist; deputy planning commissioner of Monnet Plan, 1946–1948; secretary-general of OEEC, 1948–1955; adviser to French foreign minister Christian Pineau in Rome Treaty negotiations, 1956–1957.

Marshall, George U.S. Army chief of staff, 1939–1945; U.S. secretary of state, 1947–1949; secretary of defense, 1950–1951.

Mayer, René French economics and finance minister, 1947–1948; justice minister 1949–1951; prime minister, January–February 1953; president of ECSC High Authority, 1955–1957.

Mendès-France, Pierre French prime minister, 1954–1955.

Mitterrand, François French president, 1981–1995.

Mollet, Guy French prime minister, 1956–1957.

Monnet, Jean Head of Monnet Plan, 1946–1952; head of French delegation to Schuman Plan negotiations, 1950–1951; president of ECSC High Authority, 1952–1955; head of Action Committee for the United States of Europe, 1955–1975.

Pinay, Antoine French prime minister, 1952; foreign minister, 1955–1956.

Pineau, Christian French foreign minister, 1956–1958.

Pleven, René French prime minister, 1950–1951, 1951–1952; national defense minister, 1949–1950, 1952–1954.

Schumacher, Kurt Leader of German Social Democratic party, 1946–1952.

Schuman, Robert French minister of finance, 1946–1947; prime minister, 1947–1948; foreign minister, 1948–1953.

Spaak, Paul-Henri Belgian prime minister, 1946, 1947–1949; first president of UN General Assembly, 1946; presided over ECSC Common Assembly, 1952–1953; foreign minister, 1954–1958; at Messina Conference in 1955, appointed chair of intergovernmental committee charged to study atomic energy and common market proposals, which resulted in Spaak Report.

Spinelli, Altiero Italian resistance fighter during World War II; founder of European Federalist Movement in 1943 and one of its prominent spokesmen throughout 1940s and 1950s.

Stalin, Joseph Soviet premier and general secretary of Soviet Communist party, 1922–1953.

Thatcher, Margaret British prime minister, 1979–1990.

Truman, Harry U.S. president, 1945–1953.

Uri, Pierre French economist; member of Planning Commission of Monnet Plan, 1946–1952; director general of Economics Division of ECSC High Authority, 1952–1959; drafter of Treaties of Rome, 1956–1957.

von der Groeben, Hans West German Foreign Office official, 1953–1958; drafter of Treaties of Rome, 1956–1957.

Vyshinsky, Andrei Soviet deputy foreign minister, 1940–1949; foreign minister, 1949–1953.

A Chronology of European Integration (1945–1963)

1945 *May 9:* World War II ends in Europe.

1946 *March 5:* Churchill's "iron curtain" speech.

September 19: Churchill's "United States of Europe" speech.

1947 *January 14:* Monnet Plan adopted by the French government.

March 12: Truman Doctrine announced.

June 5: Marshall Plan announced.

1948 *January 22:* Bevin's speech on the need for a Western defensive alliance.

March 17: Treaty of Brussels signed (France, Britain, and the Benelux countries).

April 1: Foreign Assistance Act of 1948 (Economic Cooperation Act) creating the Marshall Plan (formally named the European Recovery Program) signed by Truman.

April 16: Organization for European Economic Cooperation (OEEC) established.

May 7–11: Congress of Europe held in The Hague.

1949 *April 4:* North Atlantic Treaty Organization (NATO) established.

May 5: Treaty of Westminster, creating the Council of Europe, signed.

1950 *May 9:* Schuman Declaration, calling for the pooling of French and German coal and steel resources and markets, announced.

May 23: Monnet and Adenauer meet in Bonn to discuss the Schuman Plan.

June 20: Negotiations chaired by Monnet to create a coal and steel community begin.

June 25: Korean War begins.

October 24: Pleven Plan for a European defense community (EDC) announced.

1951 *April 18:* Treaty of Paris, establishing the European Coal and Steel Community (ECSC), signed by France, West Germany, Italy, Belgium, the Netherlands, and Luxembourg ("the Six").

June 3: Eisenhower's speech calling for the political and economic integration of Europe.

1952 *May 27:* Treaty establishing the European Defense Community (EDC) signed.

August 10: ECSC launched in Luxembourg.

December 11: Beyen Plan to establish a customs union announced.

1954 *August 30:* French National Assembly fails to ratify EDC treaty.

October 23: Paris Accords creating the Western European Union (WEU) signed; amends the 1948 Treaty of Brussels to include Italy and West Germany and facilitated West German membership in NATO.

1955 *May 5:* West Germany joins NATO.

June 1–2: Messina Conference to revive European integration.

June 26: First meeting of Spaak's intergovernmental committee.

October 13: Monnet's Action Committee for the United States of Europe launched.

1956 *January 19:* Adenauer directs his cabinet to support European integration.

May 29: Venice Conference approves Spaak Committee's recommendation that dual objectives of sectoral integration (atomic energy) and integration of whole economies (a common market and customs union) be created in separate organizations and treaties.

1957 *March 25:* Treaties of Rome, establishing the European Economic Community (EEC) and the European Atomic Energy Community (Euratom), signed by the Six.

1958 *January 1:* EEC and Euratom launched.

January 7: Walter Hallstein becomes first president of EEC Commission.

1959 *January 1:* First steps taken in the progressive elimination of EEC customs duties and quotas.

1960 *January 4:* Stockholm Convention, establishing the European Free Trade Association (EFTA), signed.

December 19–20: EEC's Council of Ministers approves the basic principles governing the common agricultural policy (CAP).

1961 *July–August:* Britain (together with Norway, Ireland, and Denmark) applies to join the EEC.

November 2: De Gaulle proposes the Fouchet Plan for a European political community.

1962 *January 1:* Second stage in the transition to the EEC's common market begins.

July 4: Kennedy's "Grand Design" for transatlantic relations speech.

1963 *January 14:* De Gaulle vetoes Britain's application for EEC membership.

January 22: De Gaulle and Adenauer sign French-German Treaty of Friendship and Reconciliation (Elysée Treaty).

Questions for Consideration

1. What role did the failure of the League of Nations and the European leaders to avert the Second World War play in the thinking of the pioneers of integration?
2. Why were the postwar leaders willing to experiment with international communities whose institutions were governed by supranational decision-making procedures?
3. How important to the process of European integration was the provision of American aid through the Marshall Plan and regional security through the North Atlantic Treaty Organization (NATO)?
4. Do you think European integration would have taken place if the United States and the Soviet Union had not been locked in a cold war? Why or why not?
5. What did the pioneers of integration learn from their experiments with various kinds of communities in the 1950s, especially the European Coal and Steel Community (ECSC), and the controversy over the proposed European Defense Community (EDC)?
6. Why do you think the Rome Treaty negotiations succeeded just twelve years after the end of the Second World War? Which factors—economics, security, politics, international climate, shifting balance of power, or fear of instability—were the most important in motivating leaders and statesmen to further European integration?
7. What made the institutions of the European Economic Community (EEC) different from other international organizations? To what extent did the pioneers of integration consider their initiatives unique?
8. Why did the European Atomic Energy Community (Euratom) fail to become as important as the EEC in furthering integration?
9. Why did U.S. government leaders strongly support European integration?
10. Identify the documents that show the Americans and Europeans had differing views of the Atlantic partnership. What are the differences?

11. Why do you think French leaders and statesmen took the lead in pressing for closer European cooperation and integration?
12. What was the significance of the Franco-German Treaty of Friendship and Reconciliation signed by de Gaulle and Adenauer?

Selected Bibliography

Bloch-Lainé, François, and Jean Bouvier. *La France Restaurée, 1944–1954: Dialogue sur les choix d'une modernisation.* Paris: Fayard, 1986.

Bossuat, Gérard. *Faire l'Europe sans défaire la France.* Brussels: P.I.E.-Peter Lang, 2005.

Brinkley, Douglas, and Clifford Hackett, eds. *Jean Monnet: The Path to European Unity.* New York: St. Martin's Press, 1991.

Calleo, David P. *Europe's Future: The Grand Alternatives.* Pittsburgh: Horizon Press, 1965.

Camps, Miriam. *European Unification in the 1960s: From the Veto to the Crisis.* New York: McGraw-Hill, 1966.

Cazes, Bernard, and Philippe Mioche. *Modernisation ou Decadence.* Aix-en-Provence: Publications de l'Université de Provence, 1990.

Cogan, Charles G. *Charles de Gaulle: A Brief Biography with Documents.* Boston: Bedford/St. Martin's, 1996.

———. *Oldest Allies, Guarded Friends: The United States and France since 1940.* Westport, Conn.: Praeger, 1994.

Diebold, William, Jr. *The Schuman Plan: A Study in Economic Cooperation, 1950–1959.* New York: Praeger, 1959.

Dinan, Desmond. *Ever Closer Union: An Introduction to European Integration.* 3rd ed. Boulder, Colo.: Lynne Rienner, 2005.

———, ed. *Origins and Evolution of the European Union.* Oxford: Oxford University Press, 2006.

Dumoulin, Michel. *Spaak.* Brussels: Editions Racine, 1999.

Fransen, Frederic J. *The Supranational Politics of Jean Monnet: Ideas and Origins of the European Community.* Westport, Conn.: Greenwood Press, 2001.

Gaddis, John Lewis. *Strategies of Containment: A Critical Appraisal of American National Security Policy during the Cold War.* Oxford: Oxford University Press, 2005.

Gerbet, Pierre. *La construction de l'Europe.* Rev. ed. Paris: Imprimerie National, 1994.

Giauque, Jeffrey Glen. *Grand Designs and Visions of Unity: The Atlantic Powers and the Reorganization of Western Europe, 1955–1963.* Chapel Hill: University of North Carolina Press, 1998.

Gillingham, John. *European Integration, 1950–2003.* Cambridge: Cambridge University Press, 2003.
Graglia, Piero S. *L'Unione europea.* 2nd ed. Bologna: Il Mulino, 2002.
Grosser, Alfred. "France and Germany: A Confrontation," in *France Defeats the EDC*, ed. Daniel Lerner and Raymond Aron. New York: Praeger, 1957.
Hackett, Clifford P., ed. *Monnet and the Americans: The Father of a United Europe and His U.S. Supporters.* Washington, D.C.: Jean Monnet Council, 1995.
Hoffmann, Stanley. "The Effects of World War II on French Society and Politics." *French Historical Studies*, 2 (Spring 1961): 28–63.
———. *The European Sisyphus.* Boulder, Colo.: Westview, 1991.
Hitchcock, William I. *The Struggle for Europe, 1945–2002.* New York: Doubleday, 2002.
Judt, Tony. *Postwar: A History of Europe since 1945.* New York: Penguin, 2005.
Kaplan, Lawrence S. *NATO and the United States: The Enduring Alliance.* Boston: Twayne, 1988.
Kuisel, Richard F. *Capitalism and the State in Modern France.* Cambridge: Cambridge University Press, 1981.
Lieshout, Robert. *The Struggle for the Organization of Europe.* Cheltenham: Edward Elgar, 1999.
Lipgens, Walter, and Wilfried Loth. *Documents on the History of European Integration*, Vol. 4. Berlin: Walter de Gruyter, 1991.
Ludlow, Piers. *Dealing with Britain: The Six and the First Membership Application.* Cambridge: Cambridge University Press, 2002.
Lundestad, Geir. *"Empire" by Integration: The United States and European Integration, 1945–1997.* Oxford: Oxford University Press, 1998.
Maier, Charles S., and Gunter Bischof, eds. *The Marshall Plan and Germany.* New York: Berg, 1991.
Mayne, Richard. *The Recovery of Europe, 1945–1973.* New York: Harper & Row, 1970.
Mélandri, Pierre. *Les États-Unis face a l'unification européene.* Paris: Pedone, 1980.
Milward, Alan. *The Rise and Fall of a National Strategy, 1945–1963: The UK and the European Community*, Vol. 1. London: Frank Cass, 2002.
Mioche, Philippe. *Le Plan Monnet: Genese et Elaboration, 1941–1947.* Paris: Publications de la Sorbonne, 1987.
Moravcsik, Andrew, ed. *Europe without Illusions.* Lanham, Md.: University Press of America, 2005.
Parsons, Craig. *A Certain Idea of Europe.* Ithaca, N.Y.: Cornell University Press, 2003.
Poidevin, Raymond. *Robert Schuman, homme d'état, 1886–1963.* Paris: Imprimerie Nationale, 1986.

Roussel, Eric. *Charles de Gaulle*. Paris: Broché, 2002.
Schwabe, Klaus. "L'Allemagne, Adenauer, et l'option de l'intégration a l'ouest." In *Le Plan Schuman dans l'histoire*, ed. Andreas Wilkens. Brussels: Complexe, 2004.
Soutou, Georges-Henri. *L'alliance uncertaine: Les rapports politico-stratégiques franco-allemands, 1954–1996*. Paris: Fayard, 1996.
———. "France and the Cold War, 1944–1963." *Diplomacy and Statecraft*, 12, no. 4 (October 2001): 35–52.
Spragia, Alberta, ed. *Euro-politics*. Washington, D.C.: Brookings Institution, 1993.
Stirk, Peter M. R. *A History of European Integration since 1914*. London: Pinter, 1996.
Trachtenberg, Marc. *A Constructed Peace: The Making of the European Settlement, 1945–1963*. Princeton, N.J.: Princeton University Press, 1999.
Vaisse, Maurice. *La grandeur: Politique étrangère du général de Gaulle, 1958–1969*. Paris: Fayard, 1998.
Varsori, Antonio. "Euratom, une organization qui echappé à Jean Monnet." In *Jean Monnet, l'Europe et les chemins de la Paix*, ed. Gérard Bossuat and Andreas Wilkins. Paris: Publications de la Sorbonne, 1999.
Wallace, Helen, William Wallace, and Mark Pollack, eds. *Policy-Making in the European Communities*. Oxford: Oxford University Press, 2005.

The study of the EU has been greatly enhanced by online archives created by many institutions. The following Web sites are particularly helpful to students and include many historical documents such as treaties in English. Some of them also contain photos, cartoons, commentaries, and maps as well as documents relating to current policies. The European Union's official Web site: http://europa.eu/; Historical Archives of the European Communities, European University Institute (Florence): http://www.iue.it/ECArchives/EN/; Archive of European Integration (University of Pittsburgh): http://aei.pitt.edu; History of the European Union (University of Leiden): http://www.eu-history.leidenuniv.nl/; and the multimedia Web site of ENA European Navigator (Centre Virtuel de la Connaissance sur l'Europe, Luxembourg): http://www.ena.lu/mce.cfm. Several volumes of the *Foreign Relations of the United States (FRUS)* from the Truman and Eisenhower administrations and many for the Kennedy administration are online at http://www.state.gov/r/pa/ho/frus/c1716.htm.

Acknowledgments (continued from p. ii)

Documents 1, 2, and 15: Reprinted with permission of Walter de Gruyter.

Documents 3, 13, 16, 21, and 30: From *Memoirs* by Jean Monnet, Introduction by George W. Ball, translated by Richard Mayne, copyright © 1978 by Doubleday, a division of Random House, Inc. Used by permission of Doubleday, a division of Random House, Inc.

Documents 4 and 5: Reproduced with permission of Curtis Brown Ltd., London, on behalf of The Estate of Winston Churchill. Copyright Winston S. Churchill.

Documents 9, 11, and 33: Reprinted by permission of Editions Robert Laffont.

Document 10: *Parliamentary Debates,* Commons, 5th ser., v. 446

Documents 12, 19, 22, 28, and 29: Reprinted with the permission of the Fondation Jean Monnet pour l'Europe, Lausanne, Switzerland.

Documents 14, 20, and 34: From *The Continuing Battle* by Paul-Henri Spaak. Copyright © 1969 by Libraire Artheme Fayard. By permission of Little, Brown and Co., Inc.

Document 24: Reprinted with the permission of *Vital Speeches of the Day.*

Document 25: Anjo G. Harryvan and Jan van der Harst, *Documents on European Union,* 1997, Palgrave Macmillan. Reproduced with permission of Palgrave Macmillan.

Documents 31 and 42: Stiftung Bundeskanzler-Adenauer-Haus, Konrad-Adenauer-Str. 8c, 53604 Bad Honnef, Germany.

Document 37: Reprinted with the permission of the Trustees of the Harold Macmillan Archive.

Document 41: Reprinted by permission from *Political Science Quarterly,* 78 (June 1963): 161–78.

Map 1: From Martin Gilbert, *Routledge Atlas of Russian History,* Third Edition, Copyright © Martin Gilbert. Reproduced by permission of Taylor & Francis Books UK.

Index